Insurgent Play

Insurgent Play

Social Worlds of Urban Disruption

Duncan McDuie-Ra
Monash University, Malaysia

ANTHEM PRESS

Anthem Press
An imprint of Wimbledon Publishing Company
www.anthempress.com

This edition first published in UK and USA 2025
by ANTHEM PRESS
75–76 Blackfriars Road, London SE1 8HA, UK
or PO Box 9779, London SW19 7ZG, UK
and
244 Madison Ave #116, New York, NY 10016, USA

British Library Cataloguing-in-Publication Data
A catalogue record for this book is available from the British Library.

Library of Congress Cataloging-in-Publication Data: 2025931860
A catalog record for this book has been requested.

Cover credit: Duncan McDuie-Ra

ISBN-13: 978-1-83999-346-6
ISBN-10: 1-83999-346-4

This title is also available as an e-book.

For Kimeri, who brings all spaces to life.

CONTENTS

FIGURES

ACKNOWLEDGEMENTS

This is a short book with a singular purpose, to put the concept of insurgent play out there and see what comes back. But short books still take time, feedback, discipline, clarity – all of which were hard to come by in major university administrative roles, serving on the Australian Research Council College of Experts, and in the midst of moving countries from Australia to Malaysia. Time to gather these thoughts was only possible through the generosity of visiting stints at the Asia Research Institute at the National University of Singapore, the Max Planck Institute for Social Anthropology in Halle, Germany, and the Faculty of Social Sciences at Tampere University. Thank you so much for having me.

Thank you to the following friends and colleagues for feedback on the idea at the heart of this book: Andy McDowell, Antti Wallin, Bani Gill, Benjamin Duester, Brian Glenney, Chris Giamarino, Elaine Lynn-Ee Ho, Ghassan Hage, Helena Leino, Indigo Willing, James Sidaway, Jason Campbell, Jason Cons, Kalervo Slugger Gulson, Markus Laine, Mikko Kyrönviita, Paul O'Connor, Rishabh Raghavan, Salla Jokela, Sanne Mestrom and the Art/Play/Risk project at the University of Sydney, Tim Bunnell, Tom Critchley, Ursula Rao, Vantte Lindevall.

Thanks to all my friends who play, repair and disrupt things, especially LOD, Jim, Jamie, Jas, Nash, Karl WP, Lidds and Marcus.

Special thank you to Luke O'Donnell for letting me use some beautiful photos of insurgent play around Newcastle and central New South Wales.

Extra special thank you to my family. Thanks for being radically attuned across three generations.

Chapter 1

INSURGENT PLAY

Tanjong Pagar Fitness Corner, in the southern edge of central Singapore, adjoining Yan Kit Playfield, is a well-planned play space. Activities are varied but circumscribed, surveillance is prominent and notified, target users span different age ranges and its location adjacent to several high-rise housing developments, both public and private, makes it popular with residents. The fitness corner and playfield are covered in signs. On the ground are painted images of skateboards, scooters and bikes inside a prohibition sign, and the same image is featured on elevated signs at eye level, along with the words: 'NO RIDING' (Figure 1.1). There are prohibition signs featuring a human figure climbing, a human figure kicking a ball, a detached human hand feeding a cat, a bird and what appears to be a deer. On a sign that reads 'Free to Play' are prohibition signs advising no food, no smoking, no littering and 'care for your neighbourhood' depicted by a speaker emanating sound waves (Figure 1.2). Throughout the site are a different set of signs themed 'Active Health' offering information prompts on physical activity, nutrition, sleep and screen time. One advises users about the benefits of switching off gadgets an hour before bedtime, another advises against drinking caffeine six hours before sleep, another gives information on the benefits of walking for stress relief (Figure 1.1). All feature QR codes to scan for further information.

A small running and walking track loops around the site and on the painted surface is more health information, such as 'RUN FOR YOUR LIVES! You need at least 150 minutes of exercise a week' and 'LOOK UP! Don't let your phone spoil a good walk'. While looking up (as advised), users can see surveillance cameras affixed to lighting poles, as well as signage advising of 24-hour surveillance. Scattered around the area are QR codes that users can scan to report a fault, gesturing to the norms of resident 'place-keeping' in Singapore's shared spaces (Gopalakrishnan & Chong, 2020).

The culmination of prescribed uses, prohibited uses, passive surveillance (cameras), active surveillance (QR codes) and general citizen improvement information is common in Singapore, given the technocratic planning that

Figure 1.1 Active Health but 'NO RIDING'. Photo: McDuie-Ra.

affixes identity, health, citizenship and prosperity to public space (Han, 2017; Henderson, 2013; Shatkin, 2014). And while Singapore might seem like an extreme example, similar levels of prescription, surveillance and cohesion are evident in all manner of cities appearing in various forms, languages and codes.

Far more surprising is the site of insurgent play a few kilometres away next to the Li Ka Shing Library at Singapore Management University. A long concrete ledge extends out from the wide six-stair staircase and onto busy Queen Street. A small section of the right angle of the ledge where the vertical

Figure 1.2 'Free to Play' at certain times, in certain weather and without eating, littering, smoking or making too much noise. Photo: McDuie-Ra.

and horizontal surfaces meet has been rubbed with a coarse brush, often called a 'rub-brick', to smooth the surface, as can be seen by the darker shade on the surface in Figure 1.3. Clear acrylic paint and wax have been added to make the surface easier to slide or grind with a skateboard.

On a Wednesday afternoon in May 2023, close to dusk, I sat on a marble block at the top of the stairs and watched three skateboarders attempt tricks on this ledge. The skaters looked to be in their late teens to mid-20s. I didn't ask. They didn't have the time. I knew they had a specific slice of time to

Figure 1.3 The ledge outside the Li Ka Shing Library. Photo: McDuie-Ra.

play before someone stopped them. They took turns trying different tricks on the ledge. While one attempted a trick, the other two looked back towards the library building, presumably the direction where a security guard would emerge. Rolling at high speed, bodies and boards left the flat surface and connected with the ledge, but they were all having difficulties staying on the ledge, spilling out onto the pavement after each try. Pedestrians passing on the pavement veered closer to the road to stay out of the way. After about ten minutes, one member of the trio landed a trick, a roll-on five-o grind (grinding on the rear steel truck or axle of the skateboard) before dropping into the street and rolling along the pavement. The other two hooted with joy. One raised their arms in triumph. After a few more tries, one member of the trio looked back towards the library building and they picked up their skateboards and walked through the plaza and into the creeping darkness. A few moments later, a security guard appeared, looked towards where they disappeared and then walked the other way.

The ledge is not nestled in the back blocks; it's near the intersection of two very busy downtown roads, Queen Street and Bras Basah Road, a central zone in one of the most purportedly controlled, ordered and surveilled cities on earth (Lee & Lee, 2023; Jiow & Morales, 2015; Yeo, 2023). The site is opposite the mid-nineteenth-century Cathedral of the Good Shepherd, a busy site for worshippers and tourists. Just one block to the southeast is Chijmes, an upscale dining area built in a converted nineteenth-century heritage building, and behind that is the historic Raffles Hotel, one of Singapore's most famous landmarks. Tanjong Pagar Fitness Corner is to be expected in a highly developed, meticulously planned city. Li Ka Shing ledge is totally unexpected in the same city for the same reasons. These two sites offer an extreme contrast: ordered versus disruptive, planned versus improvised, permanent versus fleeting, sanctioned versus insurgent.

The somatic expression by the skateboarders is an example of insurgent play. At some point in time, the ledge was discovered by skateboarders, its surfaces and dimensions analysed, its potential for play discussed – but not too widely or loudly. Later, likely after dark, the surface was rubbed smooth, coated with clear acrylic and slicked with wax. Modification is one step in the claim on this space; somatic acts are the second. When bodies and boards are speeding towards, along, through and off the ledge, the space is brought to life in rhythms counter to the vehicular and foot traffic and counter to the intended use. When bodies and boards are not there, which is most of the time, the traces of wear along the surface are the only evidence of the claim and resonate with only a small number of passers-by. Property owners will have a greater sense of these counterrhythms and the best ways to interrupt them are by restoring dominant rhythms, restoring order and halting damage. In other words, by practising counterinsurgency. This opening contrast also offers a further insight: if insurgent play can exist here in ordered Singapore, it can exist anywhere.

In this book, I propose insurgent play as a concept for identifying and analysing lively bodily expressions enmeshed in the constant making, unmaking and remaking of the city. In introducing and exploring the concept, I make four arguments in this book. First, insurgent play is a bodily expression that can challenge, disrupt and transgress dominant ways of city-making. The 'counter' in the counterpolitics of play is multifarious; play challenges access (and denial), amenities (and lack thereof), property rights, surveillance, fences, walls, the denial of mobility, the imposition of order.

Second, insurgent play takes us to parts of the urban landscape that we might not otherwise go, politics we might not otherwise recognise and encounters we might otherwise overlook. The concept expands the sites where we look for counterpolitics, the tools we use to identify and engage with them, the acts that might constitute claim-making, the traces these acts leave behind and the diverse and divergent agents of these politics.

Third, claims on the city made through insurgent play enliven urban space through transformative power. In this way, these claims territorialise patches of the city intended for other uses or that have fallen out of use entirely. Insurgent play is about time spent pursuing play in ways that disrupt and challenge urban orders while also generating social worlds, communities and identities. Engaging with recent advances in the study of territory, insurgent play is a way of feeling, living and acting that is temporal as much as spatial. The temporalities of insurgent play are often fragmented, but this too is part of the irregular rhythms known to players.

Fourth, insurgent play space is generated from below, never above. Insurgent play shapes, and is shaped by, identities that position adherents in opposition to prevailing urban orders, their antecedents and their remnants. Insurgence is a way of being, and the desire for insurgent play cannot be placated by better urban planning or formal expertise. Nor will multiplying designated play spaces, creative precincts and 'flexible' public spaces stop people seeking out space to create their own worlds of disruption.

The remainder of this chapter goes into detail on the two concepts being brought together, 'play' and 'insurgence', followed by an outline of the remaining chapters.

Play

Play is intrinsic to existence. We can think of play in different ways: as creative and destructive, as individual and collective, as production and consumption, as organised and spontaneous, as conformist and rebellious. Play is a preoccupation of scholars in many disciplines, from anthropology to educational psychology, and fields from media studies to urban studies. Outside the academy, it is part of corporate culture as a cultivatable stimulant for innovation and an anathema for stress, low productivity and a lack of creativity (Bateson & Martin, 2013). Play is part of protest movements (Shepard, 2012), acts of resistance (Cervi & Divon, 2023; Matyczyk, 2022), challenges to hegemonic identities and sexualities and public displays of pride (Currans, 2017). Virtual play creates and connects worlds within worlds, creating community (Pearce, 2009), and new ways of thinking about politics (Bos, 2023), architecture (Walz, 2010) and nature (Chang, 2019).

In this book, I focus on the relationships between play and the urban landscape outdoors, rather than indoor play or virtual play (discussed briefly at the end of this section). The *where* and *when* of play, space and time are crucial questions for thinking about cities, past, contemporary and future. Play is a consideration in design, architecture and planning at various scales, from obvious endeavours like playgrounds and fields to playable digital applications (Nijholt, 2017) and mobility systems such as e-scooters (Wallius et al., 2022). Beyond planned and designated play spaces, the form of the city itself invites play and always has. As Rodrigo Pérez de Arce writes, '[l]atent in the city there are endless potentials for play, just as latent in ludic practices there are potential field forms. Reciprocity characterises the interchanges between play and its grounds' (2018: 15). However, city planners, authorities and residents have varied ideas about where and when play *should* happen and who *should* be able to do it. And these ideas are constantly fluctuating.

In the 2020s, play is loosely connected to ideas about viable urban life (Ashtari & de Lange, 2019). The so-called 'new urban agenda' is framed by the United Nations Sustainable Development Goal 11 (SDG 11). SDG 11 aspires to make cities 'inclusive, safe, resilient and sustainable', focusing on public spaces (discussed in more detail below). Goal 11.7 reads: 'by 2030, provide universal access to safe, inclusive and accessible, green and public spaces, particularly for women and children, older persons and persons with disabilities' (UN DESA, n.d). Not all public space is space to play, but the general norm is that as sustainable, healthy settlements, cities need spaces that are open to participation, open to improvisation and open to all.

Once norms about the where and when of play are unmoored from narrow ideas about the volume and proximity of designated play space (playgrounds, sports fields, public pools), provocative threads emerge. There is a thread of ideas connecting play to public space and public space to better cities. There is a thread connecting play to creativity, and in turn to creative cities, innovation hubs, creative precincts and city branding. And a thread that connects play to acts of resistance, protest and pride and in turn to the spaces where these acts happen and where they are celebrated, challenged and countered. Insurgent play pulls at these threads. However, the where and when of insurgent play centres on disruption, on play in spaces and at times, that counter the prevailing order. Further, insurgent play is more covert than overt, its politics manifest in counterclaims on space.

Before going into depth on insurgence, it is important to find a workable definition of play. Most work on play begins by building upon or challenging Johan Huizinga's *Homo Ludens* (1955). Huizinga argues that play is universal to the human condition and transcends cultural, historical and civilisational boundaries. For Huizinga, play is primordial, absolute, undeniable and part of non-human animal life too. He writes, 'play cannot be denied. You can deny, if you like, nearly all abstractions: justice, beauty, truth, goodness, mind, God. You can deny seriousness, but not play' (1955: 3). Play shows us life beyond rationality, 'interwoven' with culture, and 'one of the main bases for civilisation' (1955: 5). Huizinga sees play and seriousness as interrelated. The more serious culture and society become, the more play is marginalised. The loss of play is a loss of culture, of dignity, of civilization (see Stelzer, 2023). There are scores, perhaps hundreds, of works that have revisited Huizinga since the publication of *Homo Ludens* in 1938,[1] and regardless of the degree of celebration or critique, *Homo Ludens* is identified as a foundational twentieth-century work.

Thomas Henricks offers an in-depth analysis of the play literature in chapter 1 of *Play and the Human Condition* (2015). Henricks remarks that, unsurprisingly, definitions of play vary by discipline and period, and there are substantial variations in the activities labelled play and the settings where play happens. Henricks foregrounds the paradoxes recognised in much of the literature: play is essential and unproductive, serious and mischievous, rule-bound and improvised (2015: 19). Henricks argues that most play scholars habitually aggregate its traits (2015: 35), producing mostly similar, broad definitions while also maintaining that play is difficult to define (see Sutton-Smith, 1997/2009). As a way of drawing together themes in the literature, Henricks puts forth six 'lenses' for studying play: play as action, as interaction, as activity, as disposition, as experience, as context. Rather than follow this path or regurgitate Henricks's deep critical review, I will move into the work of Miguel Sicart's *Play Matters* (2014), which gives us an affective, vitalist way of thinking about play, more 'call to arms' than thorough reckoning with past studies.

Unbound by the weighty responsibility of precise or functional definitions, Sicart opts instead to reach for a deep ontology of play and playfulness: '[t]o play is to be in the world. Playing is a form of understanding what surrounds us and who we are, and a way of engaging with others. Play is a mode of being human' (2014: 1). Sicart argues that most ways of approaching play remain bound to models derived from Huizinga and by the creep of play into education, commercial and corporate culture. Sicart's call to arms is

---

1 *Homo Ludens* was first published in Dutch in 1938. The first English version was published in 1950. The version commonly available is from 1955, though various editions have been published since.

predicated on stripping away formalised understandings, and to 'reclaim play as a way of expression, a way of engaging with the world—not as an activity of consumption but as an activity of production' (2014: 5).

Sicart gives play a vitality intrinsic to existence: 'like literature, art, song, and dance; like politics and love and math, play is a way of engaging and expressing our being in the world' (2014: 5). As expression, play is creative and destructive, individual and collective, manifest in games but also outside games in 'a tangled world of people, things, spaces, and cultures' (2014: 6). This tangled world is the 'ecology of play' in a particular context (varied in scale). The ecology of play includes the 'agents, situations, spaces, times, and technologies involved in playing' (2014: 43–44).

Taking this loose approach to questions of space, Sicart draws a crucial distinction between 'game space' – spaces designed for a specific activity of set of activities, and 'play space' – spaces where play happens with no designation or prescription. Sicart writes (2014: 51),

> [t]he size, measure, props, and even location are all created with the purpose of staging games. A game space can be created with the purpose of satisfying just one game, like some football stadiums in Europe, or with the purpose of supporting a multiplicity of games, like the old Roman arenas. Of course, the fact that game spaces are designed for games does not prevent them from being turned into play spaces. Again, play spaces are created when a space is appropriated through play.

So, play space, for Sicart, refers to 'a location specifically created to accommodate play but does not impose any particular type of play, set of activities, purpose, or goal or reward structure' (2014: 15). Sicart offers a playground as a typical example. Designated play spaces such as playgrounds may host a variety of improvisations and have variations in form, materials, condition, access, prescriptions and rules and surveillance, but at their core there is little ambiguity about what they are for, who they are for and what is expected of human bodies in these spaces. Play in designated play spaces is uncontroversial provided bodies play where they are supposed to within a range of somatic expressions. When bodies behave outside this range, or the wrong bodies intrude on the space (wrong age, wrong race, wrong gender, wrong appearance), there can be opposition from bystanders, community members, authorities and contracted security, often alerted by surveillance tools. Insurgent play is not just the wrong play but play in the wrong space.

In planned cities or smaller planned enclaves, whether public or privately developed, play *seems* to happen in designated spaces: schoolyards, sports fields, parks, beaches, plazas, pools, playgrounds and so on, whether these spaces are granted, bequeathed, legislated, mandated or won. And to encourage play, to harness the dynamism it purportedly brings to cities, the provision of play space is an integral part of planning for new developments, during renewal, gentrification and post-industrial remediation. In neighbourhoods where play space exists, strategies shift to preservation and even heritage designation (Chang & Mah, 2021). In cities with limited outdoor space or hostile weather conditions, play moves indoors in a staggering variety of forms and modes/barriers of access beyond the scope of this book.

If we take only these basic conditions, namely planned spaces designated for play or where play is allowed, with some degree of maintenance, with some provision of safety for users, and try to identify them in *and across* cities globally, these basic conditions are rare. They may not be rare in certain countries or transnational regions, northern Europe and Singapore for example, or in certain planned or 'hyper-planned' neighbourhoods, districts or enclaves within otherwise unruly cities (Braier & Yacobi, 2017). However, for most urban dwellers these conditions are not common, guaranteed nor likely. As Figure 1.4 shows, a dearth of play spaces in the city of Gangtok in Sikkim, India, means that play competes with other uses of rare open spaces, this one on top of a multilevel indoor market.

United Nations SDG data on 'open public space' is useful to illustrate the point. Open public space is not the same as play space, yet the two concepts are entangled. As Vikas Mehta argues, public space has an important ludic dimension. Mehta writes (2022: 31),

Figure 1.4 Play as a claim on space amidst other claims, Gangtok, Sikkim, India. Photo: McDuie-Ra.

Public space is a place where people come to play, to celebrate, and to let go. Play, in public, particularly for youth and adults, is a means for self- or group-expression. It is a way to be social and to enjoy public space, but play is also used as an expression of power and rights to space. For the young or those with modest resources or other restrictions, that limit their access to the city, play in public space is a way to actively engage with space and claim it for fun and display. But play is also empowering because it grants the right to occupy a part of the city.

The existence of public space tends to be a prerequisite for designated public play space (designated play space may also be private) and is a useful proxy for illustrative purposes. The UN definition of public space in SDG 11 is *very* inclusive and uses a four-part typology: (i) streets (publicly owned and maintained inside cities and neighbourhoods), (ii) open public spaces, (iii) public facilities and (iv) public commercial spaces (UN-Habitat, 2018: 9). Of these, open public spaces vary but 'can broadly include parks, gardens, play-grounds, public beaches, riverbanks and waterfronts. These spaces are also available to all without charge and are normally publicly owned and main-tained' (UN-Habitat, 2018: 10). These are further categorised by scale and size: local/pocket, neighbourhood, district, regional, national/metropolitan. Designated public play space is likely to be within these categories of open public space.

United Nations SDG data on open public space suggests there is very little of it. Of 1,072 cities in 120 countries reporting on SDG 11.7 in 2020, more than *three-quarters*, somewhere between 800 and 850 cities, have less than 20 per cent of their area dedicated to open public spaces (UN DESA, 2023). This is half the proportion recommended under SDG 11. Even more telling, on average across all 1,072 reporting cities, open public space accounts for 3.2 per cent of total urban land area (UN DESA, 2023). Granted, this doesn't tell us about designated *play* space with precision, but if we assume that open public space either encompasses designated play space or has substantial overlaps, then planned, designated play spaces are rare for most urban dwellers globally. Even if we have doubts about this correlation between open public space and designated play space or believe the sample size of cities in the UN reporting is too small, it seems unlikely that there are enough unaccounted play spaces entirely outside this definition, and of such a significant area of land, that these indicators are completely invalid. To put it simply, open public space where play is possible is a small component of urban area globally. The idealised form presented as the norm is in fact the exception.

Of course, this depends on where one is standing. In cities where the majority – or even a significant minority – of people have access to open public space within a five-minute walk, the idealised form *is* the norm. In most other cities, and for most other people, access to the idealised form is the exception. Furthermore, this data tells us only about the existence of open public space, not the quality of the space, accessibility and demand, limitations tackled by scholars in various regional, national and city-level studies (for an illustrative sample, see Anguelovski et al., 2018; Gupta et al., 2016; Rigolon et al., 2018; Wu & Kim, 2021; Venter et al., 2020). The existence of space doesn't make it accessible or even desirable. Space might be nominally public but might be difficult to access safely for children, for older persons, for persons with disabilities, for certain ethnic and racial groups, for women, for trans and other minority genders, for same-sex couples in some contexts, for mixed-sex couples in others (Arjmand, 2016; Hyra, 2017; McDowell, 1983; Nawratek & Mehan, 2020; Ruddick, 1996). Beyond access, the bodies occupying the space bring different responses from those charged with surveillance, whether public authorities like the police or private authorities like security guards, and from bystanders and other users of the space (discussed further in Chapter 4). This is heightened when bodies are racialised. The racialisation of bodies can be very localised; the wrong body in one neighbourhood might be the right body in another. And these boundaries shift constantly as neighbourhoods and commercial areas churn through demographic change from gentrification, immigration, decline, renewal, conflict and flight, resettlement and retribution. Therefore, the right body a decade ago might end up being the wrong body in the present.

Outdoor play is public, visible and just as the racial characteristics of the bodies themselves matter for access and surveillance, so too does bodily expression. Certain expressions are deemed threatening – noisy, irregular, risky, too fast, not fast enough – and can limit access, intensify surveillance or deter others. Material factors matter too. The space may be in terrible condition, covered with trash, vermin, debris or rubble. The space might be proximate to areas considered threatening. In cities, or areas within cities, impacted by armed conflict, by gang and organised crime activity or by aggressive tactics by police, military and paramilitary, open space may exist, but access is risky, even deadly, and play is out of the question.

Here we are contending with two limitations. First, there is not enough open public space in which to play. Second, the public space that does exist may not be playable, at least not for all. So, what do people do? If play is intrinsic to human existence, well-being and dignity, and if play enlivens cities, sparking creativity, innovation and civic engagement, *where* and *when* do most people do it? My argument in this book is that most people play where and when they are not supposed to – in space they appropriate and claim.

Sicart does mention appropriation briefly and uses skateboarders, the focus of later chapters of this book, as an example. Sicart writes, 'we should not underestimate the capacity of play to appropriate the world outside the environment we create for it' (2014: 55). Sicart makes a brief mention of the way skateboarders find play space in otherwise mundane 'public environments', even when cities build expensive skateparks and designated spaces where skateboarding is permitted (2014: 55). While Sicart is open to appropriation in the search for play space, appropriation is left dangling. To return to the point above, if play depends upon open public space or some approximation, then countless neighbourhoods, districts and even entire cities are bereft of play space the world over. If, on the other hand, play space is anywhere appropriated by users for play, then it is seemingly ubiquitous but requires a different analytical lens to identify, explore, celebrate and critique. Insurgent play is that lens.

Quentin Stevens's (2007) *The Ludic City* provides an excellent starting point for thinking about play and appropriation in everyday urban settings. For Stevens, because play involves 'impractical and socially unredemptive activities which are often unanticipated by designers, managers and other users' (2007: 1), it gives alternative meanings, uses and values to otherwise carefully planned and often highly prized urban spaces. Stevens identifies common urban settings where the dialectics of play can be observed: paths (pavements, sidewalks), intersections, boundaries (material, social), thresholds and props (urban objects). Stevens argues that the frequency of unsanctioned play in these settings suggests cities can be better served by inviting rather than sanctioning play, best achieved by shifting planning and design from amenity to playfulness.

To achieve this shift, urban design needs to be 'loose'. Uses and users should not be overdetermined, and planning and design should be 'incremental and open-ended, flexible and reworkable' (2007: 197). Spaces should go beyond functionality or 'amenity' (what actions and experiences are desirable and how physical environments make these outcomes possible), to embrace 'playfulness' – openness to human 'spontaneity, fickleness, willfulness, disorderliness, difficulty and danger' (2007: 216) in a variety of forms.

At the end of the book, Stevens writes (2007: 219),

[i]n truly public spaces, there will always be vagaries, flexibilities and conflicts; all have their merits. For cities to be vital, urban design needs to recognize the unfunctional and the fleeting, the partial and the uncertain; and to be provocative and invite exploration, by admitting overlap, exposure, doubt and risk.

The Ludic City opens the scholarship of play and urban space to new possibilities by breaking the reification of play space in parks, playgrounds and game space. Stevens takes seriously the everyday play that happens in public space against planned uses.

Nevertheless, the pathway to change outlined in *The Ludic City* depends upon a sophisticated approach to planning by prioritising 'loose space'. Stevens argues for minimal designation in public space to allow affordances for play. This is a very appealing approach, a sort of permitted messiness. The 'loose' spaces encouraged by Stevens will produce far better possibilities for play than over-planned and overdetermined public spaces. Such an approach requires planners to see the city differently, to listen differently and to plan differently. The solution rests on skilled professionals with a generous outlook, an openness to participation from community groups and citizens and a willingness to upset amenity. However, even if such professionals are in abundance, the success of this approach depends on there being spaces for these professionals to plan. In the cities explored in Stevens's work in Australia (Melbourne and Brisbane), the United States (New York) and Germany (Berlin), there are highly developed systems for planning, zoning, regulation, legislation, consultation and participation. These are cities where planning *happens*, so to speak, and where public space is demonstrably public. Yet as stressed above, in most cities public spaces are limited. There is not enough and likely will never be enough to sate the desire to play. Play doesn't wait for planning, and this is where insurgent play offers a different lens.

It is worth noting that cities are also 'playable' as virtual arenas in gaming, digital mapping applications and various platform interfaces (Ash & Gallacher, 2011). Gaming presents cities in a vast range of forms, from city-building games where players plan, build and sustain imaginary urban environments such as *SimCity* (Bereitschaft, 2016) to games which use real-world cities as settings for play, particularly in non-linear open-world virtual environments where players are free to explore (Denham and Spokes, 2021). Research suggests that immersion in virtual reproductions of real-world landscapes does allow them to be enrolled in mental maps, in the learning of geography (Pingel, 2018). Yet there are limits too. Pablo Fraile-Jurado (2024) argues that despite the careful and often spectacular reproduction of cities in open-world games, the primary goal of developers is entertainment, not geographical accuracy. Furthermore, 'video games also give players a sense of power and control over the spatial form of the landscape', and thus 'reflect the moral ideologies of their producers and, therefore, limit or direct the types of lessons about the real world that players can learn' (2024: 892). To put it another way, there is likely some crossover and blurring between how the city is played in the virtual realm and how some players approach the city in the material realm. There are even games where players can simulate insurgent play, skateboarding in famous urban landscapes around the world (Martin, 2013). And while valuable for thinking about cities and play, virtual play is not discussed any further in this book, which focuses on the material city and disruption to imposed order.

Insurgence

Insurgence has been prefixed to various concepts in recent decades, from planning to citizenship, from infrastructure to public space. In their work on insurgent citizenship in Brazil, James Holston defines insurgence as 'a process that's an acting counter, a counterpolitics, that destabilises the present and renders it fragile, defamiliarising the coherence with which it usually presents itself' (2007: 34). Christian Lund (2021) uses insurgence in a similar way in work on urban property in Indonesia – Bandung specifically. Lund argues that 'a fixation on government recognized private property blinds us to other relevant forms of acquisition of space, ways of securing access to land, and recognition and legalisation of claims, livelihoods, and residence' (2021: 127). And to this, I would add claims for play space: crucial for expression, sociality and belonging.

In the late 2000s, planning scholars brought the concept of insurgent planning to a range of diverse empirical contexts. Faranak Miraftab labels insurgent planning as 'radical planning practices that respond to neoliberal specifics of dominance through inclusion' (2009: 33). Miraftab continues (2009: 33),

> [i]nsurgent planning practices are characterized as counter-hegemonic, transgressive and imaginative. They are counter-hegemonic in that they destabilize the normalized order of things; they transgress time and place by locating historical memory and transnational conscious-ness at the heart of their practices.

These imaginations, these worlds, created through counterpolitics encompass an almost limitless range of counterpolitical processes including (among others): dwelling rights (Jabareen & Switat, 2019), occupation and anti-eviction practices (García-Lamarca, 2017), community infrastructure (Lemanski, 2020), DIY repair and care (Bryson et al. 2023), memorials (McDuie-Ra, 2016), art (Summers, 2022) and insurgent interventions into participatory planning and deliberative democracy (Laskey & Nicholls, 2019). Other studies have focused on insurgence from elites (Kumar, 2021), self-builders (Brakke, 2023) and the tensions and exclusions within insurgent practice (Meth, 2010).

Others still have identified quieter counterpolitics, including Jeffrey Hou's influential work on insurgent public space.

For Hou, insurgent public space is made from below through individual and group action, seeking 'place and expressions in the contemporary city and in doing so, redefine the boundaries, meanings, and instrumentality of public space' (2010: 14). Hou details a range of diverse actions, which 'may seem small and insignificant' yet these same qualities make these actions, these claims, commonplace (2010: 15). Hou outlines a six-part typology 'of actions and practices' that characterise alternative ways of creating public space (2010: 13–14): appropriating, reclaiming, pluralizing, transgressing, uncovering, contesting.[2]

Hou adds (2010: 15),

> [b]ecause of the scale and mode of production, the making of this alternative public space is more participatory and spontaneous, and therefore more open and inclusive. The insurgent public space that they have created is therefore both a smaller and a grander public space. These smaller yet grander public spaces reflect the subjectivity of its multiple actors and the broader instrumentality of space as a vehicle for a wider variety of individual and collective actions.

Public spaces made through the counterpolitical actions and practices outlined by Hou bring cities to life in new and unpredictable ways, and, further, they hold the promise for civic renewal. On this, Hou writes, '[t]hrough the variety of actions and practices, insurgent public space enables the participation and actions of individuals and groups in renewing the city as an arena of civic exchanges and debates' (2010: 16). Hou adds, 'the presence and making of insurgent public space serves as barometer of the democratic well-being and inclusiveness of our present society' (2010: 16).

The potential for civic renewal is underpinned by a normative conception of public space that veers away (though not completely) from appropriations

---

2 Hou's six-part typology in more detail:

    a. Appropriating: actions and practices that suspend the 'meaning, ownership, and structure of official public space' for different periods of time;

    b. Reclaiming: reusing abandoned or underutilised spaces 'for new and collective functions and instrumentality';

    c. Pluralising: transforming the meaning, functions and uses of space;

    d. Transgressing: infringing upon or crossing boundaries between public and private by claiming and occupying space;

    e. Uncovering: rediscovering or making space through reinterpretation 'of hidden or latent meanings and memories';

    f. Contesting: meanings, rights, access and exclusions in the public realm.

misaligned with civic virtue. Appropriations for loitering, peddling, soliciting, graffiti and play are vital to urban counterpolitics, yet don't always get us closer to a better tomorrow. Often these acts simply disrupt. Disruption may be for rational purposes, to achieve a certain outcome or challenge a specific actor or system of power. However, disruption may also be for the hell of it. And in disruption comes joy.

Insurgent play makes play space by disrupting the existing urban order. All the six actions and practices listed by Hou have the potential for disruption. Yet when the purpose is play, acts of disruption lack precision and perhaps even categorisation. Bodies at play seek somatic expression; they seek what Richard Shusterman (1999) has termed 'somaesthetics', sensory perceptions registered by the body on the one hand, and the experience of the body 'within' on the other. Seeking these experiences disrupts imposed order through calculation and, just as frequently, spontaneity.

Cities are in a constant struggle against disruption. Disruptions to transit and data systems, electricity supply, water pipes and so on manifest at the street level in delayed buses, scrambled screens, blackouts, sunken pavements and soaked sidewalks. Stephen Graham argues that disruptions to infrastructure systems 'provide important heuristic devices or learning opportunities through which critical social science can excavate the politics of urban life, technology, or infrastructure in ways that are rarely possible when such systems are functioning normally' (2010b: 3). Disruption and normalcy are relative functions, and in many cities, especially (but not exclusively) in the Global South, disruption *is* the norm. Urban dwellers have different strategies for contending with disruption depending on shared experience (Amin, 2014), shared expectations (Rupp, 2016), local politics (Arefin, 2019) and the role of fixers and other informal actors who step in when things breakdown (Degani, 2022). Cities are also disrupted purposefully, such as the shutdown of internet by governments to disrupt protests (Bächtold, 2023; Mare, 2020; Sahoo, 2023); the shutdown of various systems to deal with supply-demand imbalances (Harris, 2021; Kazmi et al., 2019); the closure of systems and infrastructure (or purposeful disinvestment) during armed conflict, emergencies or prolonged separatist struggles (Elden, 2013); the purposeful imposition of disruption through checkpoints and barriers (Baumann, 2019); and lockdowns during public health crises (McDuie-Ra et al., 2024).

Receiving much less attention are small-scale disruptions. At the scale of neighbourhood, zone, street, block or lot, disruptions are caused by humans: a sofa dumped on the pavement, improvised wires tapping the electricity lines, corn stalks planted in a vacant lot, various bodily claims on sidewalks (Loukaitou-Sideris & Ehrenfeucht, 2011). Non-humans get in on the act too: flocks of pigeons dropping shit on an outdoor eating area, feral dogs patrolling a laneway allowing nothing else to pass, a 'ruderal' orchard pushing against a border wall (Stoetzer, 2018), tree roots that raise once-flat pavement into gnarly pyramids of concrete.

In *Lively Cities*, Maan Barua explores the ways humans, animals and plants make and disrupt everyday urban life, most notably through the mischievous disruptions to urban infrastructure by macaques in Delhi (2023: 25–35). Rather than networks, nodes joined by connectors, Barua categorises cities as 'meshworks', 'an emergent and continually shifting formation, woven and knotted by the interlacing trails of its inhabitants, with flows of commodities and infrastructure, both intended and unintended, shored up at any given juncture' (2023: 6). Meshworks are alive, constituted by movement, sentience, action, subversion and disobedience, enacted and experienced by humans and non-humans (2023: 6). Urban ethnography needs to live in these meshworks, exploring the 'lives of people and other than humans, the actions of lively materials, and the atmospheres of ambient environments, all of which enmesh, and all of which give rise to the urban as a living formation' (2023: 19).

Play is part of the meshwork. *Insurgent* play brings the city to life in places and at times unexpected, feeding and feeding off the meshwork. Insurgent play does not disrupt the entire system, but like the macaques in Delhi, insurgent play introduces variation, and 'variations are about working with (urban) form from within: subtle modifications in infrastructural rhythms, introductions of off-beats and counterpoints – all have material and micropolitical effects' (Barua, 2023: 36). There are thousands, possibly millions, of small-scale variations taking place simultaneously across an urban area.

The spontaneity of insurgent play can seem random. And at times it is. But insurgent play is also territorial. In *Animated Lands*, Brighenti and Kärrholm (2020) urge for a more novel, open-ended and pluralist way of thinking about territory. They challenge the traditional thinking of territories as 'passive backgrounds for action' and focus on the vitalism of territories, their life (2020: 4). They write, 'territorial operations always give rise to new and unexpected phenomena, with the typical suddenness that characterises all life' (2020: 4). This approach skirts close to ways of understanding place, which the authors acknowledge. They suggest that place is an assemblage of multiple territories, multiple territorial claims, often overlapping.

Brighenti and Kärrholm try to shape an open-ended concept of territory through a series of insights. First, territory 'defines space through patterns of relations' (2020: 22), rather than being understood as an object or hard fact. Territory is made and remade through relations at dramatically varied scales and degrees of visibility. And as such, territories are the 'effect of material inscriptions of social relationships', of encounters, of interactions (2020: 23).

Designated play space is visible, while insurgent play space is most effective when obscured. Second, territory is imagined, but crucially, not imaginary. As an imaginative mechanism, a human (or non-human animal) is recognised as 'an intruder or insider (or other equivalent qualification) in relation to one's territory' (2020: 24). Play is a way of imagining territory, both in designated play spaces and through insurgent claims. Inclusion and exclusion form the basis of social worlds, as will be discussed in the following chapter, they are 'partial and reversible openings and closures that enact the basic operations of the territorial machine. [...] giving birth to patterns of hegemony, control, and resistance' (2020: 24). Third, territory has both functional and expressive components, the latter being critical in play. For Brighenti and Kärrholm, the material and immaterial 'ceaselessly prolong' into one another, and technology 'amplifies these prolongations and makes them more visible and perceptible' but does not make them (2020: 25). Amplification will become clearer when the mediation of insurgent play is discussed in later chapters. Fourth, territory is bounded, as most traditional definitions also recognise. Attention to boundary making is necessary, and they write, '[o]nce established, boundaries become the object of an ongoing work of enactment, reinforcement, negation, interpretation, and negotiation' (2020: 28). And through these relations, imaginations, expressions and boundary making (and transgressing) territories are entangled with human and non-human vitality 'that brings the seemingly inert into life' (2020: 31). Thus, Barua's meshworks show the city as alive through variation and disruption; Brighenti and Kärrholm suggest ways territory is made and unmade in and through these lively conjunctures.

Conclusion

People will play, whether they have designated spaces or not. Insurgent play is not just making do in deprived circumstances. There is joy in play as disruption, in messing with the order of things, in making claims on space from below for no other reason than expression, than joy. Even in cities with abundant designated play space and/or open public space, insurgent play is still common, still desired, still relished. Bodies will rebel, no matter how progressive the planning regime, how creative the public space, how welcoming the field forms. Insurgent play brings the city to life in times and places unexpected, for fleeting moments, for episodes in regular and irregular rhythms and for sustained periods of time, making and unmaking territories of varied areas, boundaries and temporalities.

The following chapters use street skateboarding as an in-depth example to explore insurgent play and refine the concept. Skateboarding is a globalised expression of transgressive play that cuts across boundaries of class, race, gender and sexuality, making it ideal to progress the concept. Chapter 2, 'Play, Damage, Wounding', explores the relationships between insurgent play and the material and physical properties of the city. The opening section goes deeper into skateboarding as an insurgent play culture. Skateboarding makes place, makes community and makes claims on the city through seemingly unproductive acts. The second section focuses on damage, the flashpoint of insurgent play. Skateboarding damages infrastructure, property and messes with urban aesthetics. However, damage is cherished in the subculture, marking insurgent play space, making territorial claims and messing with commercial and state aesthetics. The third section discusses wounding. Skateboarders are wounded by infrastructure all the time, leaving flesh, teeth and blood on the surfaces of the city. Disrupting the city hurts, but wounding enlivens the city.

Chapter 3, 'Disruptive Repair', describes the methods skateboarders apply to material objects in the city to bring them to life. There is a rich literature on DIY repair enacted by both workers charged with repair and by citizens outside of formal labour relations, often termed 'hacking' the city. I argue that when it comes to insurgent play, repair and maintenance are hacking to enable continued disruption. Through auto-ethnographic description, this chapter outlines the processes of disruptive repair through three related acts: preparing, mending/caring and fabricating.

Chapter 4, 'Counterinsurgency', analyses the tactics, practices and objects intended to maintain control of urban space, including tactics specifically intended to counter insurgent play. The opening section discusses counterinsurgent urbanism more generally, including policing and hostile design. The second section focuses on surveillance, with a specific focus on the surveillance of urban space itself and the bodies that move through it, dwell in it, claim it, play with it, disrupt it. I focus on the rhythms and counterrhythms of surveillance and insurgent play. The third section analyses counterinsurgent objects, specifically the 'skatestoppers', an umbrella term for objects installed on surfaces of the city to prevent insurgent play. Skatestoppers have become ubiquitous urban objects, promising aesthetic order, social order and anticipatory order. The final section of the chapter explores public and covert activism against counterinsurgency, territorial struggles over the right to disrupt the city.

Chapter 5, 'Under the Flyover', weaves the argument of the book back through an ethnographic account of the most prototypical insurgent play spaces: the underside of flyovers. Flyovers are cast, and demanded, as a solution to density. Whether coveted or reviled, all flyovers have an underside. The underside of flyovers provides obscured patches for insurgent play. Concrete pillars, angled drains, supporting walls can all be utilised to make insurgent play space, along with fabricated ramps, bumps and pilfered street objects. DIY assemblages are enclaves for play, hidden zones of expression away from the rest of the city. DIYs can also be thought of as a territorial form. Established by claiming space, DIYs grow through voluntary labour, social rhythms, codes of belonging and patterns of exclusion, disrupting dominant modes of city-making.

Chapter 2

PLAY, DAMAGE, WOUNDING

Street skateboarding, skateboarding in the open public spaces of cities globally and outside designated skateparks, is a compelling example of insurgent play. Street skateboarders make play space out of the surfaces and objects of the city. Figure 2.1 is a typical example. The photograph shows insurgent play in action. Here the skateboarder, 'JM' (pseudonym), has rolled down the asphalt street, onto the concrete driveway, onto the sandstone wall (a trick called a 'wallie' or 'wallride' depending on how it is executed). That is the moment captured in this photograph. In the next moment, 'JM' will pop off the wall onto the pavement and then roll at high speed down the steep street to the bottom of the hill.

Behind the walls are an electricity substation and associated office buildings. The compound is nestled in a residential area. There are houses further up the hill out of the frame, apartment buildings and a synagogue on the opposite side of the street. It is an 'ordinary street', yet the surfaces and angles make it desired as play space and subject to claims by the skaters. The changing surface of the wall makes it particularly desirable. A close look at the lower portion of the sandstone wall, just below where 'JM' is positioned in the photo, shows textured sandstone blocks, which are too rough to ride on, and skaters must land on the wall above these blocks and leave the wall before rolling down onto them. The (somewhat) levelled driveway breaks the trajectory of the steep pavement, allowing skateboarders a flat roll-up to the wall. The steep hill is part of the draw too. Trying to stay on the board while rolling at high speeds down the hill is part of the challenge and where the exhilaration really kicks in. A trick on the wall is one accomplishment; holding the roll-away down the hill is another. This space is not designed for play. The assemblage is a happy accident for skateboarders and meaningless for everyone else as a combination of surfaces, angles, surveillance cameras, designated speed limits, no parking notifications and street trees.

There is more to the photograph. It is a social world. To the right of the frame, another skateboarder 'S' (pseudonym) is making his way back up the

Figure 2.1 'JM' wallie and roll down the hill. Photo: L O'Donnell, used with permission.

hill. 'S' has had a turn skating the wall, rode to the bottom of the hill and is now returning to a mark just outside the frame to take his next turn. To the far left of the frame, another member of the group can be seen sitting on a skateboard filming 'JM' with a video camera. Out of frame, at the bottom of the hill and at the intersection with an adjoining side street, other members of the group are stationed to stop any vehicles that might turn onto the steep street. These 'spotters' are crucial to controlling the flow of vehicles into the space but also for communicating that the road is clear before one of the skateboarders pushes off. As the session goes on, these roles switch around. Someone else will pick up the camera, someone will go from skateboarding to spotting and so on. And for a few hours, this zone becomes an insurgent play space.

Close up, the wall has traces of skateboarder wheels, scuff marks from the edge of the wooden board, steel bolts and shoes. These traces of damage are an integral part of insurgent play. They signal to others that the wall can be skated, that it has been initiated (see Vivoni, 2013). Damage also infuriates property owners, municipal authorities and other citizens, though this depends on the space and its location in the city, as will be discussed below. And the space has potential for wounding. There are so many ways to hurt oneself at this spot: miscalculating the angle to hit the wall and falling forward, or back, onto the pavement; getting 'speed wobbles' on the downhill roll and falling – skin and bones first – onto the road or pavement (or both) at high speed; rolling onto a rock or seed pod from the trees that line the street and falling onto the road or pavement and even colliding with a vehicle that slips past the spotters.

This photograph is typical of moments of insurgent play in cities the world over: somatic, expressive acts on surfaces and objects assembled in desired ways in spaces identified through well-honed attunements to urban space for potential play. These acts disrupt intended uses and acceptable flows of the city, building social worlds through shared attraction to disruption. The surfaces and objects in this zone are brought to life in new ways in these moments, through these counterclaims. Damage leaves traces behind, marks territory, and wounding or the potential for wounding, constitute claims on space. Risk emboldens bodies, and the more steps taken to stop disruption and restore order, the more emboldened these bodies become.

This chapter establishes street skateboarding as an exemplar for insurgent play by first focusing on 'radical attunement' to the built environment, a concept described in various ways emerging from advances in literature on skateboarding and urban play in the last two decades. The following sections detail three sensory attunements in turn: desire, damage, wounding. Taken together, these attunements hint at the kinds of spaces coveted for insurgent play.

Radical Attunement

Skateboarding prides itself on radical inclusion. As a subculture that encompasses somatic, cultural (art, music), media (photography and video) and social worlds, skateboarding has tended to vacuum up the outsiders, whether voluntary or forced, in different geographical contexts (Borden, 2001: 140–42). Exclusion, when it happens, is based on a failure to share the ethos of skateboarding subculture rather than established social fissures like race, gender, class, age. In recent years, this founding belief has been criticised, raising two divergent points of view. First, despite being a subculture (i.e. distinguished by non-normativity, but not necessarily norm-less, see Gelder, 2005: 6), skateboarding might not be very inclusive at all. Second, and conversely, skateboarding has a long history of diversity across boundaries of race (Atencio et al., 2013; McDuie-Ra, 2023a; Williams, 2020), gender (Abulhawa, 2020; Fok & O'Connor, 2021; Yochim, 2009), sexuality (Carr, 2017; Geckle & Shaw, 2022), age (O'Connor, 2018; Willing et al., 2019) and class (Dinces, 2011).

Depending on the geographic and sociocultural contexts where scholars draw their empirical material, skateboarding comes off as either less inclusive than imagined or more inclusive than credited. And both perspectives are probably evident depending on where one goes looking (for discussion, see

McDuie-Ra, 2023a). The contextual nature of outsider-ness makes it difficult to make assumptions on inclusion and exclusion in skateboarding that apply across time and space; 1970s California is different from 2010s Bangkok, to state the obvious. The racial, gendered, sexual and aged composition of these worlds depends on *where* they are formed, though empirical research has not travelled as fast or as far as the subculture (McDuie-Ra, 2021a; 2021b; 2023a).

I mention inclusion and exclusion upfront because it is a flashpoint in both internal and external readings of skateboarding subculture. I do not mean to suggest representation doesn't matter. It does. However, skateboarding research can get caught up in the celebration or condemnation of inclusion in the subculture, which, while interesting to subculture diehards, limits the potential of research on skateboarding in provoking questions about urban social worlds. As discussed below, there is a shift underway, with more scholars drawn to the lively, affective properties of skateboarding, returning to some of the ideas introduced in foundational works, such as Borden's *Skateboarding and the City: Body and Space* (2001).

Appreciating what skateboarders *do* draws us to the ways bodies and senses are attuned to the city, and the ways skateboarders create social worlds in doing, in playing, in disrupting worlds that entangle spaces and make territories. In keeping with this shift, in this book I am primarily (but not exclusively) interested in what skateboarders *do*, rather than what they *are*, or what people would like them to be, shifting focus from radical inclusion (and its deficits) to *radical attunement*.

Insurgent play generally, and skateboarding in this case, commands attunement to field forms of the city. Attunement to our surrounding environment shapes the ways our attention is drawn to certain things, while other things go without notice (Throop & Duranti, 2015). When we enter unfamiliar spaces or territories, we notice objects, colours, movements, rhythms, tastes, sounds and smells that might be taken for granted by occupants and regular visitors familiar with the space. As Throop writes, '[t]o speak of the world is thus not to speak of a homogenized and singular totality but to speak instead of variegated intensities, aspects, situations, events, and horizons that are continuously unfolding, in flux, and shifting' (2018: 203). At the same time, there may be things that stand out – breaking the 'norm' – and draw the attention only of people who are familiar with that social world. Throop adds (2018: 203),

> [m]oreover, while we may willingly focus our attention on a particular aspect of our world, our noticings may also always be directed and redirected by the actions or responses of others who variously engage that world with us, by the objects, events, and activities that transpire within

it, by the affects, sensibilities, and moods that we inhabit and inhabit us, and by our habitual orientations, dispositions, and expectations.

So, as our bodies move through the city, our affective and sensory attunements vary, yet there are certain attunements that are shared among particular social worlds, subcultures and somatic crafts. Shared attunements are not totalities of experience but relate to certain atmospheres, objects and surfaces.

Skateboarders are attuned to assemblages of material objects, surfaces, inclines, drops, voids that would otherwise go unnoticed or unremarked by other urban dwellers. Their attunement is radical in *where* and *what* is desired for play and in challenging dominant uses and users. Skateboarding brings different rhythms to urban space (Borden, 2001). Crucially, these rhythms are not just rhythms of speedy flow. For outside observers, a skateboarder rolling past at speed along a pavement is one kind of rhythm, one somatic form. However, as play, skateboarding has multiple rhythms, including the stop-start rhythms of attempting tricks, of damage and wounding, of repair and care (Chapter 3), and the interrhythms of play during intervals and glitches in surveillance (Chapter 4).

To understand the alignment between skateboarding and insurgent play, it is vital to focus on *street* skateboarding. Street skateboarding happens in street space, not in designated skateparks.[1] Skateboarders are attuned to radical possibilities for play in street space, the grey space (O'Connor et al., 2023). In expanding on the concept of grey space, Paul O'Connor argues that 'skateboarders who play in urban space work with and derive health and well-being from polluted urban spaces' (2024: 2). O'Connor writes (2024: 2),

> Grey spaces hold the capacity to articulate that skateboarders, as purveyors of urban leisure, are at once subjects of and contributors to pollution. They are policed, excluded, and challenged in their use of urban space, seen as a social pollutant by bringing noise and disruption to the normative frame of the city as a place of commerce. They are also heirs to the unwanted, toxic, and dangerous parts of the city and are frequently used as a tool to cleanse and gentrify spaces.

---

1 There is a small part of skateboarding that is competition-based, but it is just that, small and is not part of this book. Competition has an outsized presence among casual observers through televised events, like the Olympic Games and various 'extreme' sports. These take place in designated play spaces and thus don't help with exploring insurgent play space. There is an adjacent literature on this world, see Bäckström & Blackman, 2022; Lorr, 2005; Thorpe & Wheaton, 2011; Williams, 2022.

As a descriptor of a type of urban space, grey space is brilliant in directing our focus away from designated play spaces planned to capture creativity, activity and, as O'Connor references, even gentrification (see also Howell, 2005; O'Keeffe & Jenkins, 2022), and towards the greater urban malaise where acts of insurgent play find their home.

While there is a proliferation in public skateparks as stand-alone play spaces, like public space more generally, these tend to be concentrated in certain cities and regions of the world. Of note, Glenney and O'Connor argue that contemporary skatepark designers 'replicate plazas, urban civic centres, parks and shopping malls [...] [T]he very same areas which skateboarders have been excluded from' (2019: 847). Often a skatepark will include replicas of famous objects from insurgent play spaces. Figures 2.2 and 2.3 show an example from Newcastle, Australia, a city with a rich skateboarding history. Figure 2.2 shows the original spot, a downward ledge, also referred to as a 'hubba' in skateboarding culture, outside the library and art gallery. The hubba is famous among local and visiting skateboarders. The newly renovated Newcastle skatepark, opened in mid-2024, features a scaled-down replica of the hubba as a tribute to the original (Figure 2.3). The object made famous by insurgent play is now integrated into the design of the legal, designated play space, itself part of the city's counterinsurgent strategy (see Chapter 3).

Figure 2.2 The original marble 'hubba' (downward ledge) outside the Newcastle library and art gallery. Photo: McDuie-Ra.

Figure 2.3 Scaled-down replica of the hubba in the Newcastle skatepark. Photo: McDuie-Ra.

An increase in skateparks does not diminish the appeal of play in the streets. One of the great mysteries to urban planners and municipal authorities is why skateboarders won't stay in the expensive skateparks made for them (Chiu, 2009). Many skateboarders resent being herded into contained spaces, even if they appreciate the existence of skateparks in their city. And an increase in skateparks is often accompanied by a resultant crackdown on skateboarding in other parts of the city.

However, there is much more to it than that. First, skateparks mute the attunement described above. A critical part of skateboarding's ethos is the capacity of skateboarders to sense, discover and appropriate space designed and built for other purposes. Brian Glenney (2023), building on the idea of polluted leisure, argues that skateboarders demonstrate enskilment to polluted spaces. Glenney writes, 'those adept at navigating polluted spaces unconsciously move their body, manipulate their environment, and socialize with their community in different ways, producing modifications in their senses, skills, and satisfaction' (2023: 4). He adds, '[e]nskilment is particularly suited to skateboarding whose senses orbit the body's balance coupled with its visual and imaginary attunement to urban spaces to form a multimodal sense' (2023: 5). This sensory attunement pinpoints possibilities for creativity and somatic expression from found space and otherwise mundane urban objects. Sensory attunement to the objects and surfaces of the city has also been termed the 'skater gaze' (McDuie-Ra, 2021a). Shared by skaters across time and space, the skater gaze is attuned to the possibilities for extraordinary bodily performances from otherwise mundane patches of infrastructure.

Second, skateparks lack the thrill of disruption. Authenticity and legitimacy in skateboarding subculture are based upon what's done in the streets, in the grey spaces. It is based on risk, apprehension and escape. Furthermore, relationships between bodies, boards and material surfaces of the city are fundamental to the somaesthetics of skateboarding (see Chapter 1). With this focus in mind, for the remainder of the book I will drop the 'street' from street skateboarding and 'street' skateboarder; when I write 'skateboarding', I mean skateboarding in the streets, skateboarding outside designated, legal play spaces.

Insurgent play is recorded as image and video, circulated using digital media, and consumed, emulated and imitated across time and space; it is part of the 'ecology of play' to recall Sicart (2014: 43). Capturing media is secondary to the sensory experience of play but adds to the variegated topologies of street space. The capture and circulation of skateboarding as image and video give insurgent play a volumetric, topological quality. In this way, skateboard media captured in city streets is a form of 'cultural topology', what Roger Shields calls a way of identifying a new '"dimensionality" regarding spatial and temporal relations, flows and transformations' (2013: 159). Maan Barua articulates the differences in effects between typologies, which 'divide worlds', and topologies which 'multiply them' (2023: 144). He adds, '[a]nd in topologies lie the prospect of the advent of a different city, for another urban to come' (2023: 144). The other urban, the parallel city driven by the desire for disruption, is a provocative way to think about insurgent play.

The desire to capture play drives, in part, the appropriation of space. Skateboard media circulates and celebrates acts of disruption, encouraging more. It provides a medium for sharing appropriation tactics and practices of repair and care discussed in the following chapter. Images and footage of a particular insurgent play space draw others to the space, provided they can identify where it is. Spaces get added to digital maps, online forums, skateboarding travel guides – akin to a sort of 'dark tourism' of greyspaces – and are shared through person-to-person connections. The location of some spaces is kept deliberately obfuscated to protect them from unwanted attention.

Filming and photographing insurgent play and circulating footage and images for consumption seem risky. As argued in the previous chapter, insurgent play depends on some level of covert appropriation of space. Capture and circulation do the opposite; they showcase acts of appropriation, which might involve trespassing, damage and other infringements. Yet the risk doesn't stop the proliferation of image and video content that could give it all away.

By now I hope to have established two points in this chapter. First, as an ideal type of insurgent play, skateboarders demonstrate a radical multi-sensory attunement to the built environment, particularly the polluted or 'grey spaces' of the city. Second, the appropriation of otherwise mundane space for play, and its capture and circulation as media, draws our attention to the topologies of insurgent play, the dimensionality of urban space. Cultural topology denaturalises taken-for-granted urban categories of analysis – use, amenity, property, rules, laws – and reveals instead 'a form of city making that is improvisational' (Barua, 2023: 144), disruptive and also territorial. But what exactly are skateboarders attuned to? The following sections explore three sensory attunements that generate the social worlds of insurgent play: desire, damage, wounding.

Desire

Skateboarders desire different forms depending on their skill level, their level of risk and the kinds of tricks (expressions) they prefer. However, there are some generalisable attributes necessary for skateboarding in most cities globally. The most basic is smooth surfaces. Observing skateboarders in situ, the pull of smooth surfaces can be overwhelming. Once a skateboarder gets the feel of a smooth surface, the sensation of rolling along at speed with minimal resistance, it becomes an addiction. It can be very difficult to avoid the temptation to roll wherever possible. In cities where smooth surfaces abound, skateboarders have more choice, more control. In cities where smooth surfaces are scarce, the desire is bottled up and takes over the body when smooth, open space is near. For skateboarders in cities with rough surfaces, crowded streets, bad weather, dust and mud, smooth surfaces are magnets that pull skateboarders, such as the marble ledge in Kampong Thom, Cambodia, in Figure 2.4, the smoothest surface for miles amidst dust, mud and potholed roads.

The desire for smoothness attunes skateboarders to the surfaces of the built environment within and between cities, indexing urban development at different scales (see McDuie-Ra, 2021a). There are so many variables that produce smooth surfaces, that lead to their decline or that prevent them ever being realised. For example, in Aizawl, the capital city of the state of Mizoram in India's far eastern borderlands, the best roads are around the main commercial areas (always crowded) and connect to army bases. The region has a heavy military and paramilitary presence owing to the proximity to international borders with Myanmar and Bangladesh and decades of separatist insurgency through the 1960s to 1980s (Zou, 2010). The smoothest, quietest roads lead to the army bases, winding through the steep hill topography. And it is on these roads that I encountered skaters in Aizawl.

Figure 2.4 'Young K' in Kampong Thom, Cambodia. Riverside redevelopment creates smooth surfaces rare in this part of the country that are irresistible to skateboarders. Here 'Young K' grinds the ledge with a 'roll-on 5050'. Photo: McDuie-Ra.

On a late afternoon in 2014, two boys in their early teens were taking turns to skate down one of these roads, hill bombing one of the smoothest roads in town. The boys shared one skateboard. They were positioned at a curve in the hill so they could spot other vehicles. One would act as a spotter further up the hill, checking for oncoming vehicles and then call out to the skater stationed below to 'go!', and the skater would bomb the hill, disappearing out of sight. Ten minutes later, the skater would appear, walking up the steep hill, hand over the board and the two would switch roles. At one point, a mammoth dark-green troop transport vehicle teared around the bend headed downhill just as the skater was going. The spotter started yelling and waving his arms, and the skater took a quick look over his shoulder, jumped off the board and ran into the roadside dust; seconds later the troop carrier thundered past, horn blaring. Both boys roared with laughter and resumed their positions to start again. Here, play space is an audacious claim among complex histories of occupation and control. Two boys skateboarding down the hill, dodging military trucks, is a minor, low-stakes statement, barely noticeable during a period of relative peace, when disturbances come from trouble in neighbouring territories. Nonetheless, their hill bombing disrupts order – an order imposed by the military during some of the city's darkest years – it's a counterrhythm in the city streets – the vibrancy of bodies on boards and wheels waddling down the hill alongside the roar of massive troop carriers.

In other cities, the most desired smooth surfaces are in open public spaces such as plazas, squares, esplanades and the open spaces around stadiums, monuments and showpiece urban developments. As Setha Low has argued, the publicness of plazas 'provides a forum, or theatre, for the performance of personal, social, and cultural dramas that can be observed, recorded and analysed' (1997: 4). Skateboarding is part of this drama. Martin Place in Sydney is desired by generations of local and visiting skateboarders from other cities and countries. In Australia's urban history, Martin Place is iconic. It is a fixture of Sydney's frontstage. As Judith O'Callaghan et al. argue, '[s]ince the early twentieth century, it has held a special place in the public consciousness as the city's most meaningful civic setting for expressions of public sentiment and opinion, whether patriotic, anti-establishment, celebratory or commemorative' (2016: 30). They add, Martin Place's 'gravitational force goes well beyond its functional role as a central city transect' (2016: 30). Martin Place has deep symbolism associated with colonisation, nationalism, war, finance, modernity and later, globalisation. It has also been a site for commemoration (especially since the Cenotaph was built in 1927), nationalist spectacle, political speeches, protest,[2] 'pedestrianisation' of the city centre, public art installations and accelerated global capitalism in the 2000s with global luxury stores, hotel chains and ubiquitous brands taking over the spaces in and around the plaza (see Alić, 2016; Bogle, 2016; D'Arcy, 2016; Simon, 2016).

---

2 Dijana Alić discusses protests against the so-called 'Vietnam War' and conscription through the mid-1960s to 1970s, Indigenous rights protests in the late 1960s, protests against the APEC Summit in Sydney and the ongoing war in Iraq in 2007, and Occupy Sydney in 2011 as some pertinent examples. See Alić, 2016.

It also has many alternative histories, histories of the unhoused, of performers, of maintenance workers, including a subaltern history as insurgent play space. This history is unseen by even the most adventurous chroniclers of Martin Place. In the excellent edited collection *Sydney's Martin Place* (O'Callaghan et al., 2016) there is no mention of play generally, or skateboarding particularly, in 600 plus pages. In other circuits of culture, the plaza's life as insurgent play space is richly chronicled. The plaza has attracted skateboarders for generations, particularly since the early 1990s when street skateboarding took off in Sydney. I was in my teens in this era, and commuting to central Sydney to skate on Sundays was a common ritual. The central business area was empty on Sundays, especially before the development of malls and weekend trading. On Sundays, Martin Place felt like it belonged to skateboarders – a claim, a territory. There have been waves of crackdowns on skateboarding in Martin Place, from police patrols to private security guards, to skatestoppers on the surfaces of the most desired objects (Figure 2.5). Injections of capital, from a luxury hotel in the old post office to a new metro station, have rearranged parts of the plaza. Despite this, it has survived as insurgent play space.

Martin Place appears in hundreds of skateboarding videos and magazines. It also appears in countless personal archives of non-professional skateboarders. As such, it has been archived over decades as insurgent play space parallel to, and as a challenge to, its designated uses, symbolism and representation. In skate media, Martin Place is featured when crowded, presenting encounters with hostile citizens, zealous authorities and enraptured onlookers. By contrast, during the COVID-19 pandemic, Martin Place was almost entirely

Figure 2.5 Martin Place's iconic black hubba in 2023. An additional handrail has been installed to block the black marble surface from skaters. Photo: McDuie-Ra.

empty due to lockdowns and other restrictions across the city (McDuie-Ra et al., 2024). Yet the plaza was alive with skateboarders, epitomised in Sydney skateboarder Chima Ferguson's part in the acclaimed, multi-million viewed video *Nice to See You* (Hunt, 2021; see McDuie-Ra, 2023b)

Martin Place holds such a prominent place in skateboarding culture that a toy replica was created for the Tech Deck miniature fingerboard series (miniature toy skateboards 'ridden' using human fingers) by the Canadian company Spin Master (Figure 2.6). The replica features the famous double-sided handrails and black marble hubba, along with a depiction of the sign for the railway station. This replica exists in an entirely different world of consumption than other souvenirs of Sydney landmarks. Indeed, it is doubtful that tourism authorities, historians, architects and planners steeped in the history of Martin Place even know of its existence. It is a replica of the objects of desire for insurgents, not the beautiful aesthetics of Martin Place's prized architecture, or its role in major events of memorial, celebration and nation-building. The replica is cast in gaudy plastic – the material itself some kind of counterclaim to beautifully crafted sandstone and marble in the plaza's original design and projections of power.

Smooth surfaces can also be found in the urban backstage, in car parks and alleyways, in abandoned lots and industrial estates, in shopping strips and public works projects. The ground is the starting point, but skateboarders also desire various other field forms. Curbs, handrails, benches, embankments, walls, ledges, gaps or voids and even cracks, grates and foliage are desired by skateboarders if they hold possibilities for play. And for skateboarders, play on and through these field forms, these assemblages of surfaces, objects and angles, causes damage.

Figure 2.6 Martin Place replica. Photo: McDuie-Ra.

Damage

Skateboarding damages surfaces. Damage is sensation; it is part of the desire for specific spaces and surfaces for play. There are various terms used to refer to the sensory experience of damage. I will use 'shredding' here as it is used in skateboarding culture (though it goes in and out of popularity) and it describes the sensation for the body/board, the wear on skateboard parts and the change to the surface of objects from play. Shredding is moving along the surface of an object, especially an angled or rounded edge (a concrete block, a steel handrail, a painted concrete curb), with part of the skateboard other than the wheels (see Figure 2.8). Many skateboard tricks involve shredding and over time shredding changes the appearance and form of objects.

Chasing the sensation of shredding, of damage, brings skateboarders to a multitude of objects for play. The attractiveness of these objects is not always apparent to authorities, property owners and the public at large, though once shredded, depending on the extent of the wear, the draw of the objects is revealed. 187 Thomas Street in Haymarket, Sydney, is a famous skate spot (Figure 2.7). The puzzle at this spot is getting past the handrail bolted onto the side of the planter box to reach the angled surface and shred it to the end. Damage is clearly marked on this portion of the ledge. In Figure 2.7, evidence of a 'skatestopper' (see Chapter 4) can be seen on the concrete surface furthest

Figure 2.7 187 Thomas Street in Sydney's Chinatown (Haymarket). The photo shows the gap to clear around the handrail, the waxed surface to grind or slide and the pockmarks where 'skatestoppers' have been removed. Photos: McDuie-Ra.

away from the stairs. The skatestopper looks to have been hammered out and the bolts used to install it into the surface have been grinded down to restore surface flow – tactics to keep the spot playable, to sustain the claim.

Shredding is the epitome of disruption. Shredding disrupts the aesthetics, the form and the prescribed use of urban space. Furthermore, shredding lingers long after the act of play is over. The damage left behind attracts more play, and as such, shredding is a critical part of attunement. Skateboarders are attuned to the possibilities for shredding, for damage. And they seek spaces that offer these possibilities, identify them, claim them and mark them.

These marks are gestures to territory, spaces where skateboarders have paused long enough to leave a mark. The duration of these pauses might be a few hours, ranging to years of repeated play. In this way, marked, damaged objects stretch play time from the initial shredding to the traces left behind, to the draw of these traces for other skateboarders to use the same objects for play. This interplay of material and non-material elements, Brighenti and Kärrholm suggest (2020), amplifies territorial claims and marks the boundaries of insurgent space.

Skateboarding is towards one end of a spectrum in the correlation between insurgent play and damage. With skateboarding, damage is part of play, part of disruption, not an accident or occasional consequence. Skateboarding is thus open to the charge of vandalism. Like closely aligned subcultures including graffiti, stickering, paste-ups and acts of culture jamming (Carducci, 2006), skateboarding is a provocation, part art, part 'insurgent communication' (Iveson, 2010). Skateboarding is, arguably, graffiti as play. This is not to suggest that graffiti, stickering, paste-ups are not playful. Playfulness is inherent in the practice, the message and affect. Skateboarding, however, exhibits play as bodily movement, as somaesthetics. Whereas graffiti is secretive, skateboarding can be witnessed. And its players are not anonymous. Covert activity, especially in preparing and repairing surfaces, is an important part of the subculture, as will be discussed in Chapter 3.

However, not all insurgent play is thus, nor even most. At the opposite end of the same spectrum is insurgent play that leaves no trace at all. On a warm winter Sunday in the suburb of Cabramatta in western Sydney, groups of elder citizens, most of whom share Southeast Asian heritage, engage in insurgent play on pedestrian strips around the shops and restaurants (Figure 2.8). The local council has installed concrete forms that morph from block benches to make table-like surfaces. Men, and it is almost all men, use these surfaces to play games (often with bottle caps) on chequerboards they have drawn themselves.

Their play is a counterclaim on space too. Bodies occupy objects intended for other purposes. They do leave a trace behind, the game boards drawn

Figure 2.8 Insurgent play in Cabramatta. Photo: McDuie-Ra.

onto the concrete, guiding others who may come at another time. Though this level of damage does not seem to have attracted attention from the authorities, there are other examples like this. Acrobats and exercise groups take over empty spaces, wastelands and underutilised facilities. Dancers practise routines in the space between buildings or in alcoves to the side of underground pedestrian thoroughfares. Even the most ubiquitous insurgent play, children playing ball games in alleyways or against the outer walls of buildings, appears to leave no trace (until a window gets broken). Of course, in taking up space, in practising somatic expression that counters established urban rhythms and prescribed uses, and by making noise, the urban order is disrupted, even if there is little left behind.

Wounding

Play hurts. Bodies slam into concrete, steel and marble during play, leaving blood, flesh and teeth on the streets. Skateboarding culture celebrates wounding – part rite of passage, part accepted price to pay for using the city as playground. Stories of wounding are a constant in the social worlds of skateboarding. I am cognisant of these wounds as I write this chapter. I cannot rest my left elbow on the desk because of acute bursitis from years of falling on the same bone. My left leg must be stretched straight as I recover from a ruptured anterior cruciate ligament – injured while skateboarding in an abandoned velodrome. My injured leg makes it hard to use a standing desk, referring pain to my shoulders and neck. I periodically sip hot coffee from a mug, and when I do, I curl my lips over my top teeth, a tic I've had for most of my life after knocking my front teeth out skateboarding 35 years ago. I have reinjured my teeth twice since after hitting my head loosening the repaired dental work. My wounds are not unique. Most skateboarders carry wounds with them. It is part of the culture, a sign of dedication, perseverance and perhaps some obstinance too.

Insurgence plays an important role in wounding. In some spaces, skateboarders must try things quickly, before security guards, interventionist citizens, or, more simply, crowds make play impossible. This is a fundamental temporal difference between play in designated play space and insurgent play. Where play is designated or fits within acceptable uses, skateboarders and other players can take their time with their craft, their somatic acts. Play outside these spaces is subject to the impending threat of shut down, so skateboarders must take risks, fast, with less time to hesitate, pontificate or procrastinate. Wounding ensues. Like damage, there is a spectrum of sorts. Insurgent play at a spot on the urban frontstage, such as Martin Place, might have a short window for trying high-risk tricks. The window might be bigger at different times of the day or week – Sundays, for example, nights – but generally, insurgent play in spaces of public, state and commercial value, use and symbolism has smaller windows. Insurgent play in a rarely used car park, a vacant wasteland or under a flyover is at the other end of the spectrum, rarely subject to intervention.

Insurgent play brings the wounding potential of mundane urban space into view. Any space in the city can wound. Harris Solomon explores 'injurious infrastructures' in Mumbai, India (2021: 2), considering the relationships between mobility and wounding. He argues that the infrastructure created to facilitate the flow of bodies is also 'at the heart of the pervasive damage to everyday life' (2021: 4). In Solomon's work, wounding comes from attempts to use infrastructure as it is meant to be used. Yet infrastructure breaks down, it attacks and wounds and social inequalities have a major bearing on who gets hurt and who gets fixed (2021: 14). Solomon's work resonates here because skateboarders are wounded by infrastructure all the time – some critically. However, the key difference is that they are not injured in using the space as intended; they are wounded making counterclaims, wounded moving *against* the flows of city, not *with* them. Choosing to risk severe injury for joy, for play, is privileged wounding. The built environment doesn't attack skateboarders in so much as they attack it and in turn live with the bodily consequences.

Conclusion

Skateboarders are drawn to various field forms on the urban frontstage and backstage. Some of these are obvious. The open space, smooth granite tiles and marble ledges of the riverfront at Kampong Thom are irresistible (Figure 2.4); so too is the marble hubba outside the Newcastle library (Figure 2.2). The marble hubba is so perfect that after decades of being claimed by insurgents, it has been replicated in a designated play space built by the municipality (Figure 2.3). Martin Place in Sydney is so desired and so famous among skateboarders in Sydney and around the world that it has a toy replica as part of a series of other famous insurgent play spaces (Figures 2.5 and 2.6). There are thousands of spaces like this in cities the world over: plazas, squares, promenades, pedestrian zones, monuments and various urban renewal projects 'opening up' old industrial sites and so on. These spaces are desired for insurgent play, claimed for somatic expression, enlivened by disruption. However, skateboarders develop a radical attunement to other spaces, other field forms, assemblages of surfaces and objects that hold no obvious way of playing to people outside the subculture.

Take the two-textured wall and steep hill in Figure 2.1, for example, or the bevelled concrete edge jutting out from a set of four stairs, made even more desirable by the steel handrail bolted to part of the ledge that must be cleared to shred the end of the ledge and land on the pavement (Figure 2.7). Both need high-level skills to unlock their potential for play, and in this way, radical attunement to the possibilities for play brings thousands, possibly millions, of otherwise unremarkable, mundane spaces to life in cities globally. And this attunement, this multi-sensory desire for certain surfaces and objects, is developed and shared by skateboarders across time and space.

The desire for certain field forms sparks insurgence. Skateboarders make claims on spaces and envision these spaces as territories, territories claimed through the presence of bodies on boards across a range of time spans, short and long, sporadic and constant. Damage is part of these claims. The sensation of shredding is an overwhelming sensory experience that travels through the body as it moves 'through' the friction of wood and steel on concrete, steel and marble. Damage leaves traces of insurgent play behind; some obvious, some more subtle. These traces provoke counterinsurgent tactics from property owners, authorities and even citizens, discussed at length in Chapter 4. However, damage also archives insurgence; it leaves clues to others about alternate uses of the space, about the potential for disruption. Some of these traces are deliberately enhanced through acts of preparation, repair and care discussed in the following chapter.

All this disruption, all this expression, hurts. Wounding is an essential part of skateboarding. Unlike urban dwellers wounded attempting to move with flows of the city, skateboarders are wounded moving against intended flows. In polities where the fear of litigation following injury is pronounced, such as in the United States of America, counterinsurgent tactics are explained (and sold) as protecting the material condition of property *and* protecting against potential legal action by people injured during insurgent play. However, wounding is part of the pact skateboarders make with the city's objects and surfaces. Risk is the price of play and the quality that makes disruptive play addictive. Corralling all this risk into designated play spaces with regulations, rules and waivers numbs the thrill, hence the continued appropriation of space for play, even in cities, towns and suburbs with state-of-the-art designated play spaces, such as skateparks. Still, when viewed through a global lens, skateparks are rare. In most cities, insurgent play space is not an alternative to designated play space; it is the only play space.

Chapter 3

DISRUPTIVE REPAIR

Creating playable surfaces can be easy. Surfaces like marble rarely need any modification. Granite and other hard surfaces might just need a coat of wax applied by hand; the same goes for anything painted. Powdery surfaces, like new concrete, need a lot of preparation. In any surface, cracks and holes can be plugged if the volume of space to fill is small; otherwise, rocks and rubble need to be shoved in first. One of the most challenging surfaces is pebble-crete. Pebble-crete is very rough. The gaps between pebbles make it difficult to shred the surface with parts of the skateboard; steel trucks (axles), the wooden underside of the skateboard (deck) and the urethane wheels are no match for the thousands of tiny surfaces and angles of a pebble-crete surface. However, in certain cases, skilled repair work can make even pebble-crete playable.

The surface in Figure 3.1 is one of four patches around the edge of this emptied pond in foreshore parkland in Newcastle, Australia, known locally as '2300 Pond'. The preparation work making this surface skateable has many stages: smoothing the rough surfaces, filling thousands of gaps between the pebbles with a thick coat of Bondo,[1] adding a further layer to the top and side of the right-angled ledge, then applying clear coat or another sealant for weathering and finally wax to make it easier to skate. The work in Figure 3.1 was four years old at the time of this photograph, battered by the sun, rain and hundreds of hours of play. The Bondo work is impeccable. Adhesive tape has been used to keep a straight, clean edge. The repaired area has been painted to blend into the pebble-crete, masking the work from authorities. The masking only mattered for a while. Eventually, the repaired surfaces

---

1 The name 'Bondo' comes from a product line of synthetic body filler by 3M. The name has become the universal term for any similar product among repairers. The term is also used as a verb, for example, 'I will Bondo that crack later'.

Figure 3.1 The repaired ledge in the '2300 pond'. This photo was taken four years into its life as insurgent play space. Photo: McDuie-Ra

Figure 3.2 2300 Pond, circa 2021. Photo: McDuie-Ra.

brought more and more skateboarders to the pond, and they added more objects into the space, claiming the entire space for play, as in Figure 3.2.

By late 2021, the pond was insurgent territory. At its peak, the pond became so popular that for a time it had its own Instagram account. Skateboarders tagged the account with clips filmed at the pond, and it served as an archive of this territory, this slice of insurgent play space in the heart of the city. The space also drew people on bikes, roller-skates, scooters and tricycles. An informal timetable developed: young children in the mornings, teenagers and older people in the afternoon, drinking and loitering in the evening.

The authorities made several attempts to reclaim the territory. At one point, all the obstacles were removed. Another time, the entire pond was fenced off, stopping access. Through all this, the pebble-crete ledges remained. Blasting off the repair work with a high-pressure hose, a tactic used on other surfaces in the same city, didn't work. The pebble-crete, Bondo, clear coat and wax had merged. There was no way to break them apart. And because of this, because the edges of the pond remain skateable, tactics to reclaim the territory continued to fail. There would be a few months of quiet, then new obstacles would start to appear overnight, and the space would be brought back to life again. The pond is part of an area slated for major redevelopment, which will eventually be the end of its insurgent life. It seems only the complete destruction of the space can stop it from being claimed for insurgent play.

Repair and care by skateboarders are best identified on the surfaces of the city. These acts are a quiet celebration of surfaces as 'interfaces [that] can be productive, enlivening, and enchanting spaces, where diverse materialities meet to produce physical and aesthetic mixtures, fluidities, turbulence, and movement' (Forsyth et al., 2013: 1017). Skateboarders care and repair for surfaces and objects that range from functional to dysfunctional, newly built to ruined, on the frontstage of the city and its backstage. As described in the previous chapter, the properties of surfaces determine whether a particular space will be desired for play. Repair and care work changes the properties of surfaces, opening new play spaces and, in turn, forming the basis of territorial claims. In this chapter, I focus on three related acts: Preparing: filling, smoothing and slicking surfaces to improve flow; mending/caring: reviving prepared surfaces damaged by time, weather, tampering or counterinsurgent tactics; fabricating: creating objects and obstacles that mimic elements of the built environment, known as DIY spots in skateboarding culture. While these acts are specific to skateboarding, most types of insurgent play involve some modification work to enable disruption, work that requires an ethnographic gaze to uncover. Like all appropriations for insurgent play, they have a radically unpredictable spatio-temporality. It is difficult to anticipate where and when claims will happen and how long they will last. While some urban field forms are obviously attractive for play, many more others are only *made* attractive through intervention, acts of preparing, mending, caring and fabricating, like the peddle-crete edge of the pond.

Repair is affective, generating intimate relationships between repairers, tools and objects. Repairers are part of furtive networks with the cunning to modify cities in ways barely perceptible to the public. These networks share knowledge on techniques, tools and stratagems. Repair is empowering too, in that the city can be transformed through direct intervention, rapidly imagining play space into existence.

Cultures of Repair

Graham and Thrift have argued that repair and maintenance are ubiquitous acts that sustain modern life, the environments in which humans and other lifeforms dwell and 'are the main means by which the constant decay of the world is held off' (2007: 1). Their challenge to imagine cities as socio-technical complexes in need of, and undergoing, constant repair and maintenance is a powerful adage for thinking through unevenness within and between different polities, cities, neighbourhoods, individual dwellings and even single objects – signs, stairs, drains and the infrastructure that connects these sites and scales. Notions of caring have extended beyond the well-being of living things to the care of 'things'.

Insurgent play thrives on repair and care practices. As Shannon Mattern has argued, while political and social capital come from new infrastructure, new buildings, new precincts, new renewal projects, new uses for old spaces, the focus on the new 'obscures the phenomenal reality that the world is being fixed all around us, every day' (2018: n.p). Since the early 2000s, a branch of scholarship has focused on improvised, DIY urbanism. In *The Help-Yourself City*, Gordon Douglas discusses the ethos of DIY urbanism, mostly in the Global North, defined as 'unauthorized yet ostensibly functional and civic-minded physical alterations to the urban built environment in forms analogous (however abstractly) to official planning and streetscape design elements' (2018: 20, brackets in original). In the Global South, attention to improvised repair and care practices, networks and knowledge reveals worlds of necessary fixing as part of everyday urban life (Baptista, 2019; Barua, 2023; Kaur, 2016; Lemanski, 2020). Further, improvisation and informality by citizens enact bonds of community and citizenship (Anand, 2017; McFarlane, 2011). Much of this research focuses on the improvisational practices in neglected buildings, neighbourhoods and municipalities (Amin, 2013; Dovey, 2012; Truelove, 2021). However, as Mattern argues, 'examples of non-Western improvisation are now often adapted, appropriated, or fetishized in the West [...] [t]his can lead to the idealization of repair, the romanticization of strategies of survival, and even the recasting of austerity as a form of intellectual or moral prosperity' (2018, n.p., see also Badami, 2018).

In contrast, Kumar (2021) explores the ways improvisation for repair in Bihar, India, is as much a practice of elites as marginal denizens. In a similar vein, Müller and Trubina (2020) describe the transformation of the Yeltsin Centre in Ekaterinburg, Russia, through improvisation existing in-between tactics of the marginalised and elites. Crossover between DIY tactics and creative city imaginaries, including 'pop-up' urbanism, directs attention to improvisations for alternative or 'third' spaces, often co-opted for various gentrification projects or arts-led urban renewal (Harris, 2015; Madanipour, 2018; Martin et al., 2020). Whether originating from marginal, elite, in-between or alt-social ('creative') interests, DIY repair and care practices seek to improve infrastructure in response to public (or private) neglect or inepti-tude (Corwin & Gidwani, 2021). Function is the primary imperative, and repair and care are most successful when barely noticed (Douglas, 2018).

DIY repair and care for insurgent play seek to alter existing surfaces and objects to better enable disruption, not function. The original function of the infrastructure is not relevant. As such, DIY repair and care for insurgent play are subversive insofar as they encourage alternative uses of surfaces and objects and in turn allow for counterclaims on space. Repair and care for insurgent play are, unsurprisingly, performed outside the formal practices of public authorities, private property owners and managers, and their contrac-tors. It is often illegal, or at the least in an area of legal limbo, especially when practised in ambiguous patches of the city where the boundaries of public and private space blur.

As such, DIY urbanism resonates with 'hacking', what Sophia Maalsen calls 'small-scale, everyday negotiation of urban life', common across both the Global South and North (2022: 455). Maalsen argues that hacking can show where urban problems exist, demonstrate alternative possibilities for urban space, and, crucially, hacking produces contested outcomes; rarely unequivocally good for all (2022: 458). Maalsen writes that hacking can be co-opted by powerful actors, it can coexist with the interests of the powerful, and 'it can disrupt and show alternative futures' (2022: 457). When it comes to insurgent play, repair is hacking to enable continued disruption.

Returning to skateboarding, in this chapter I explore acts of repair, care and modification by skateboarders and identify five features that contribute to our understanding of insurgent play. First, like other insurgents, skate-boarders repair – and care for – material objects and surfaces for the use of other skateboarders, not the greater public good. Repair enables play; it creates public space and/or creates new uses of existing public space by disrupting the urban order as set out in Chapter 1. Repair and care enable disruption through play, not the smooth functioning of the city. Disruptive repair brings patches of the city to life that are otherwise moribund or reserved only for designated uses and users; they are part of the 'meshwork' of the city described by Barua, introducing variations, 'off-beats' and 'counterpoints' to established rhythms (2023: 26). Second, repair and care acts are boundary acts, a way of demarcating territory. Returning to Brighenti and Kärrholm, repair and care acts enable functional and expressive elements of territory, though the function in this case is an alternative function to that intended by planners, designers and builders. The specific techniques, surfaces and objects subject to repair for insurgent play are easy to identify for those attuned to their look, helping to buttress territorial claims made on space. Third, the less visible the repair work, the more likely it is to endure. In this instance, subtlety is key for the repairs conducted by skateboarders who do not want to attract attention to their self-governed practices, illegal modifications or to fully impede the general use of the surface or object in question, as in Figure 3.3. The location of the repair work is a major factor here; in spaces further away from public attention, subtlety is less important,

Figure 3.3 American Museum of Natural History. The waxed ledge at the entrance of the museum is in prime real estate. Photo: McDuie-Ra.

Figure 3.4 Backstage in Brooklyn. The ad hoc preparation and fabrication enliven a neglected patch of a neighbourhood park. Photo: McDuie-Ra.

as in Figure 3.4. There is a site-specific interplay between the second and third points here. Subtle repair work leads to subtle territorial claims and vice versa. Further, in spaces where repair work started out as subtle acts, the longer a space is used for insurgent play, the more difficult it is to hide the material effects of disruption. Fourth, acts of repair and care have no guarantees of longevity. Like all insurgent play space, repaired spaces are vulnerable to destruction through demolition and redevelopment, further modification through defensive architecture to deter skateboarding, and surveillance and policing (see the following chapter). Fifth, knowledge about techniques of repair and care are considered an important part of skateboard culture to be learnt and shared. This knowledge sharing crosses geographic, national and linguistic ranges. It is fascinating to observe similar repair and care practices in diverse cities across the world, suggesting a genuinely global set of practices loosely grouped into preparing, mending/caring and fabricating.

Repair in Three Acts

Acts of repair are varied; however, through my participation in repair practices, through witnessing repair acts carried out by others, from skating repaired surfaces and from immersion in cultures of repair, I group these into three main acts: preparing, mending/caring and fabricating. In the following sections, I will use 'we' when describing practices I've shared with others.

Preparing

Rough surfaces, cracks and bumps interrupt surface flow. To prepare these surfaces for play, we must smooth them out. Once a space has been identified, the first thing to look out for is surveillance, either human or electronic. Experienced repairers know where to look for surveillance technology and how to gauge whether it is activated for the surface under repair. This takes some trial and error, and we often 'test' these systems with some minor play at different times of the day or week to see what happens (see Chapter 4). Then we touch the surface, running hand palms along the surface gives a quick read of texture. The next steps are determined by that read. If the surface feels too rough to salvage, or if the space feels like a bust, then we move on. If we think it is worth preparing, then the material properties of the surface determine the next acts. Rough concrete, pebble-crete, stonework needs the most preparation, while painted surfaces, marble, metal and timber need much less.

For rough surfaces, we begin by rub-bricking. Rub-brick, a plastic-handled brush with a dense metal pad, is used to rub the concrete surface to smooth it out. It's like sandpaper for concrete. Rough surfaces can take hours to smooth out, and this is best done in episodes over different days so as not to arouse suspicion. The fine powder that comes off the surface needs to be swept away, along with dust and other debris, before the surface is sealed. We then coat the surface in clear lacquer with a brush or spray can and leave it to dry for a few days. Once dry, the surfaces that will have contact with any part of the skateboard are waxed to make them slick. Any wax will do, from a candle, paraffin, even beeswax – though softer wax can melt off the surface quickly. The combination of rub-bricking, clear coat, wax and then wear from play gives skated surfaces a distinctive grey/black marking.

Ground surfaces also need to be smoothed but only to allow wheels to roll. If they are too slick, it is difficult to grip and launch off them onto other surfaces. In preparing ground surfaces, we focus on cracks. Cracks might be on the ground surface, such as the pavement, and need to be filled to allow skaters to roll up or roll away from an object, or on the surfaces desired for shredding, such as a concrete ledge. Repairing cracks requires synthetic putty or 'body filler', commonly referred to as Bondo. After sweeping debris out of the crack and sticking electrical tape around the sides, Bondo is combined with 'hardener', usually on some cardboard or a plastic container. Once mixed, a scraper or other flat tool (we have seen a mud guard from a car used, for example) is used to lift the Bondo onto the surface and smooth it down into the crack. After the Bondo dries, we remove the tape and sand down the edges to make the Bondo blend into the surface as much as possible. The patch might even be painted (Figure 3.5).

Figure 3.5 Bondo runway. The patch of rough pavement leading up to this curved handrail has been covered in Bondo in a neat strip, a bit like a runway and painted black to throw off detection. Photo: McDuie-Ra.

Figure 3.6 Mended surface. The plugged gap and well-maintained wax coating can clearly be seen. Photo: McDuie-Ra

Mending/caring

Once in use, prepared surfaces are damaged by the act of skateboarding itself and by weather, traffic, tree roots and debris, seismic activity and therefore need to be mended (Figure 3.6). Mending is a community task. Once we notice the waxed ledge is becoming sticky, we apply some more. If there are new cracks in the surface, we will mend them with Bondo. Crucially, protocols of mending dictate that new materials should not be introduced to surfaces already claimed for insurgent play. For example, adding a metal edge or a timber top to ease sliding or grinding would be considered a violation of protocol.

By contrast, removing objects that get in the way of desired surfaces is considered acceptable. This is a trick; if removal is too obvious, it risks the attention of authorities and property owners. Though some spaces are worth the risk, even if just for a few hours of play. In some locations, removal can have surprising longevity. One of the most famous skate spots in New York City is 'blubba' or the 'black hubba'[2] – an angled marble ledge down

---

2 Hubba in skateboarding vernacular refers to a ledge angled downward, rather than protruding straight, alongside stairs or ramps without a handrail or other objects attached. The word is used globally for this kind of urban field form. The name comes

Figure 3.7 Blubba in New York. In the near frame, the black marble down-ledge still has the handrail intact. In the far frame is the hubba claimed by skateboarders with the handrail removed.[3] Photo: McDuie-Ra.

a wide, curved set of five stairs in Foley Square in downtown Manhattan, on the northern edge of the financial district (Figure 3.7). The space is remarkable as insurgent play space as it sits adjacent to the New York County Supreme Court, whose facade is a staple in television programmes and films, as is the plaza itself. Blubba is part of the Triumph of the Human Spirit monument, which has six similar black hubbas spaced around the staircase that connects the upper part of the plaza with the lower part on the north side of the monument. Blubba is famous in skateboarding subculture. Most skateboarders know it by sight, even if they have never set foot in New York City, or even the United States. There is even a short documentary about the history of the spot by *Jenkem Magazine* (Castro, 2018). In the documentary, long-time New York-based skate filmer RB Umali recalls Blubba being skated in late 1999 before the construction of the monument was even complete. The first known footage is from the classic skate video *Photosynthesis* (both Anthony

---

from a space in San Francisco dubbed 'Hubba Hideout' by skateboarders in the late 1980s and early 1990s.

3 Notably, two of the six marble hubbas have lampposts on them, which would make them very difficult to skate even if the handrail was removed.

Van Engelen and Pat Corcoran have tricks at the spot, see Castrucci, 2000). After skateboarders started to claim the space, metal handrails were installed above the marble edges, making it difficult to skate.

Over the next 20 years, footage of play at Blubba shows people skating the object with the handrails on, with them removed, with one removed and one in place. During my visit to the space in 2024, Blubba was 'free', in that there were no handrails or other skatestoppers on Blubba itself. Notably, skateboarders (and other insurgent players, such as BMX bikers) have remained focused on only one of the six hubbas, as if in silent negotiation with the city. And the space has survived for over 20 years. This is remarkable given its location on the urban frontstage and the battles over other insurgent play space in the vicinity (Chiu & Giamarino, 2019).

Caring refers to general upkeep beyond the surfaces that are skated. Care work includes removing debris, cleaning up litter and even trimming vegetation. Even if the primary imperative is disruption, once claimed, caring for space helps sustain it. Related to this, spaces of disruption attract other disruptors. And some of these disruptors make a mess. If insurgent play space looks too unruly, it will attract attention from the public, property owners and authorities. Of course, it depends on where this space is located. Skateboarders are attuned to location. They know that play space in crowded areas or areas of high income, commercial areas and sites of intensive surveillance will draw attention if they're not well cared for.

Fabricating

Fabricating is creating a new object, or part of an object, for play. DIY spaces, composed of multiple fabrications, are commonly found away from residences and active business districts, such as under bridges and flyovers, in abandoned lots and buildings and in wastelands. There is an emerging literature on DIY spots and the ways these interventions challenge dominant spatial practices and planning logic (Hollett & Vivoni, 2021; Kyrönviita & Wallin, 2022). Fabrication in spaces 'naturally' occurring in the built environment is more controversial. Any fabrication that makes a space too easy to skate is frowned upon. What exactly constitutes 'too easy' is difficult to articulate, perhaps best explained as any fabrication that alters the height or scale of a spot, whereas small fabrications that make a spot skateable that was not beforehand, such as bumps in a drainage ditch or concrete barrier, are acceptable.

Fabrication is less about modifying existing field forms and more about creating new forms that complement what already exists. The barrier in Figure 3.8 is a good example. Hidden in long grass by a riverbank, the concrete barrier was positioned at the end of a small patch of concrete opposite a fertiliser plant to stop trucks driving into the marshy ground along the riverbank. The space sits at the edge of a larger industrial zone and is only accessible through an unnamed access road that runs from the nearby cross-river bridge. Aside from trucks accessing the plant, the road is also used by people accessing the river to go fishing, and because bits of the area are obscured by the bridge and other industrial detritus, it's also used for illicit trade. It's a disorderly zone, and fabrication for insurgent play doesn't provoke any strong opposition.

Once the barrier was spotted, the ground was prepared. First, overgrown grass and weeds were shovelled out and the ground levelled to enlarge the flat surface. After using timber to create a form and nearby rocks and broken chunks of concrete to fill in the volume, hand-mixed concrete (in light, portable plastic tubs) was poured into the form work to enlarge the surface at the base of the barrier and left to dry. In the week that the concrete was left to dry, people carved tags and initials into the surface with sticks. Even the unsanctioned and probably illegal modifications to the space for play were vandalised by locals – counterclaim on top of counterclaim. The next step

Figure 3.8 Cleaning up the fabricated spot. Photo: McDuie-Ra

was creating a concrete transition onto the barrier to make it easier to skate – hand-mixed and hand-trowelled directly onto the surface. Bondo filled gaps between the new and old surface and have been applied through mending every five to six months. The spot requires constant repair, particularly after heavy rain, using brooms, shovels, rakes, garden shears and leaf blowers.

Through preparation, mending, care and fabrication this patch of the riverbank is brought to life through the sporadic rhythms of disruptive play amidst the regular rhythms of industrial warehousing and logistics, and the sporadic rhythms of recreational river use and illicit transactions. Fabrication is perhaps the strongest territorial claim for insurgent play space. By creating objects and add-ons that were not already there, this work brings new spaces into being. Fabrication goes beyond making do to simply making, in very visible, touchable, material ways.

Conclusion

Repair work for play has no guarantees. Investments in equipment and materials, time, labour and the risks of arrest or fines for unauthorised work might yield play space for a single day. Playable objects get demolished in the churn of urban development. Surfaces get worn down, weathered, destroyed in storms and earthquakes, and after neglect the labour of repair can be too great for the payoff. A repaired spot may come under new routines of surveillance triggered by skateboarding or by other illegal activity nearby. Even seemingly minor things, like new occupants in a building in proximity to the sounds, movements and social worlds of disruptive play, can lead to increased surveillance, complaints and destruction.

Creating playable space that brings dour patches of the city to life is addictive. It makes play space out of mundane space. Repair also allows the city to be imagined anew. Once repairers develop the skills to modify surfaces and objects, new possibilities for play open and spaces that are too rough, too hazardous, too sticky can be claimed for play. Transforming the city in this way is the lifeblood of street skateboarding, generating spaces for play in patches of the built environment intended for other purposes. While there are similarities with acts that seek to improve the function of cities in the face of neglect, breakdown or absence, repair and care for skateboarding seek to create new possibilities for a specific group of people and for specific activities. Despite this specificity, traces of repair and care by skateboarders can be seen in cities across the world and in skate media – photography and video – consumed by millions of skaters across the world.

Further, unlike tactical modifications that subvert governance, capitalism and surveillance through visible DIY acts, repair and care for skateboarding have the best chance of longevity when barely noticed, when the statement is muted and repairs blend into surrounding surfaces. Knowledge and techniques of repair and care are circulated directly among skaters through skate media. Beyond the knowledge itself, the expectation that skateboarders will undertake acts of repair and care is an important part of skate culture across boundaries of language, nation, race and gender. Anyone who plays, repairs and cares. Through repair and care, skateboarders alter the surfaces of the city for play, for disruption and make territorial claims on space for varied periods of time, from a few days to decades.

Chapter 4

COUNTERINSURGENCY

Newcastle Permanent is a community-based financial institution (building society in Australia) with its head office on the corner of Union and King streets in downtown Newcastle, Australia. The building itself is a brutalist masterpiece, with tiered floors finished in pebble-crete and narrow windows spanning each floor. An updated refurbishment has added a folding facade of steel and tinted glass to one part of the building, and in front is a landscaped garden with palm trees and other coastal plants housed in raised garden beds. The edges of the garden beds are topped with a layer of granite. The granite hangs out over the vertical edge of the garden beds, creating ledges for insurgent play. At the corner of the lot, the garden bed walls start low to the ground and rise upwards, a metre or so off the street level, almost making a pointed corner, a little bit like a ship's bow. The horizontal granite surfaces are covered in rows of small steel blade-like strips spaced about 30 centimetres apart from one another and rising to about 3 centimetres from the granite surface – skatestoppers.

This is a busy junction, and the traffic lights are slow. Pedestrians and drivers have a long time to look at this garden, the trees and the hundreds of steel objects covering the surfaces. In the middle of the day, office workers come and sit in the garden to eat lunch. I have watched as they arrange themselves between the steel blades to find a comfortable position. It is hard to know whether they notice these blades or know what they are for, but on surfaces in cities around the world, bodies encounter these counterinsurgent objects with seeming oblivion.

For skateboarders, the space is tantalising. Granite is a desired surface for insurgent play. It slides and grinds well and doesn't need as much modification and care work as raw concrete. The garden has ledges at different heights for varied play, and the angled ledges at the street corner are the most attractive of all. I have sat in my car at the corner and gazed at the angled ledge, daydreaming about the possibilities for tricks. Local skateboarders chat about these possibilities all the time. Yet the possibilities seem remote: the space is in the middle of a major intersection, there are surveillance cameras affixed to the outside of the building and the inimical row of steel blades stop surface flow.

Then, one day in early 2024, the blades were gone from one side of the ledge, and a coating of wax showed a darkened strip of surface all the way to the top (Figure 4.1). Chatter spread about who, when and how long this would last. And then, in February 2024, a short video featuring professional skateboarder Rowan Davis was released through the *Free Skate Magazine* online platform (McDonald, 2024). During the video, Davis is filmed speeding along King Street towards the ledge; he pops onto the ledge on the nose (front wooden part) of the skateboard and slides all the way up the ledge and as he nears the end of the ledge, he twists his body and board 270 degrees in the air and lands on the pavement in the same direction he started.

The counterinsurgent objects kept this space free of insurgent play for years. Then through covert activism to free the surface, the established order was transgressed; this corner of the city was disrupted for play, for joy and a momentary claim was made on the space. The removal of the skatestoppers brought more people to the space to play, establishing temporary rhythms, staking claims. The appearance of the ledge in an international skate video captures these claims, transmits them, encourages mimicry.

Counterinsurgency in this chapter refers to the tactics, practices and objects designed to maintain control of urban space and in the context of this book, to specifically counter transgressive acts of play. Urban counterinsurgency takes myriad forms. Capturing most attention are violent counterinsurgent tactics, humans and machines (tanks, jeeps, drones) that patrol streets, staff checkpoints and implement blockades. Most studied in militarised urban

Figure 4.1 One ledge has been liberated from counterinsurgent objects, the other has skatestoppers intact. Photo: McDuie-Ra.

environments experiencing – or emerging from – armed conflict,[1] urban counterinsurgency is also part of policing in conditions of (nominal) peace and future urban planning (Bou Akar, 2018). For example, in *Policing Los Angeles* (2018), Max Felker-Kantor charts the turns towards counterinsurgency in the Los Angeles Police Department following the Watts Uprising in 1965 through the various anti-gang, anti-drug and anti-immigrant initiatives in subsequent decades, culminating in the brutal police response to the 1992 Los Angeles Riots/Rebellion. Felker-Kantor writes that for the community in targetted neighbourhoods, 'police surveillance, harassment, arrest, and incarceration structured their daily lives and the very meaning of citizenship, race, and identity' (2018: 239). Felker-Kantor's focus on counterinsurgency in Los Angeles is instructive too as the city is perhaps the global capital for insurgent play through street skateboarding, especially during the 1980s and 1990s (see Snyder, 2017), and play is bound up in other tactics to control street space. Street skateboarding has a racially diverse history, especially in cities like Los Angeles, and the surveillance and policing of play is shaped by relationships between space, race and power in different zones of the city. This holds in other cities too, though the specific relationships are deeply contextual and best analysed through a relational lens (Goldberg, 2009).

As Stephen Graham has shown across various works, human and machinic counterinsurgency is a regular part of the urban landscape, urban planning and urban development. Urban counterinsurgency exists even without troops on the streets or physical blockages and checkpoints. Everyday urban space is, in Graham's words, 'battlespace' (2009). Insurgent play is entangled in

---

1 Including my own sole and collaborative work on counterinsurgent planning and urban development in the frontier cities of Northeast India, Imphal (McDuie-Ra, 2016) and Dimapur (Kikon & McDuie-Ra, 2021). Both cities have been shaped by counterinsurgency, occupation, inward migration from across international borders and conflict-affected regions of the countryside and the alternative urban governance structures of underground groups. Counterinsurgency characterises the built environment of these two cities and is continually being reimagined through different cycles of demographic change, capital injections and attempts to formalise municipal governance. I mention this work here to stress that I don't use counterinsurgency lightly. The experience of counterinsurgency in frontier cities is pervasive and the stakes higher than many of the episodes discussed in this chapter. However, at their core is a similar logic of order, control, surveillance and what Graham refers to as the 'interpenetrations between urbanism and militarism' (2009: 384). The point of this chapter is that great lengths are gone to counterinsurgent play. And these tactics are manifest in the everyday urban environment in visible and invisible ways. High-stakes counterinsurgent environments can teach us much about the everyday urban landscapes of nominally peaceful cities.

battlespace and invites the extension and adaption of battlespace tactics to counter.

As discussed throughout this book, insurgent play is about making claims on space by disrupting the existing order and establishing somatic rhythms that counter established rhythms and flows. Counterrhythms establish territories through vast temporal ranges of activities, from brief moments to repeated disruption to repair and modification. The most effective way to counter these claims, these rhythms, is to aggressively regulate space through hostile architecture, also referred to as hostile design. Smith and Walters identify hostile architecture as 'designed to actively exclude particular categories of person' (2018: 2983–84). They add, 'such architecture is not the result of thoughtlessness or poor planning, but rather it is a deliberate act to constrict the social field of the city' (2018: 2984). As Mike Davis famously argued in *The City of Quartz* referring to Los Angeles, 'the city is engaged in a merciless struggle to make public facilities and spaces as "unliveable" as possible for the homeless and poor' (1990: 232). Robert Rosenberger has developed a classification scheme for hostile design, and it is a valuable starting point for this chapter. Rosenberger's schema focuses on 'the ways hostile designs shut down specific uses of public space', the 'hostile functionalities' of a particular object (2023: 57). The first is physical imposition, wherein existing objects, surfaces and spaces are modified to make certain physical engagements difficult or impossible. This captures the functionality of skatestoppers perfectly; indeed, Rosenberger mentions skatestoppers in the example. It is also worth noting the other categories in the schema: sensory interference, annoying stimuli – often sound – to discourage loitering; concealment, purposeful discouragement of use for certain amenities; confederacy, objects that aid the work of human authorities, including hidden cameras discussed in the previous section; self-coercion, signage and other texts that list rules and penalties for transgression; and absence, the non-existence or removal of objects that are expected and needed in a space, such as seating, shade, toilets (2023: 57–62). Insurgent play comes up against all these. It's really only annoying sonic stimuli that has a limited effect on insurgent play, especially skateboarding, because it is so loud to begin with (see Glenney & O'Connor, 2023). The main hostile functionaries for skateboarders are surveillance and its confederate networks, and skatestoppers, the epitome of physical imposition. I will discuss these in turn before moving to activism against counterinsurgency.

Surveilling Play

Surveillance, whether human or electronic, is a vital tool in urban counterinsurgency. David Lyon defines surveillance as the 'focused, systematic and routine practices and techniques of attention, for purposes of influence, management, protection or direction', that 'occurs as a 'normal' part of everyday life in all societies' (2007: 14). When it comes to surveillance and urban space, it is useful to distinguish between surveillance of individual behaviour through abstracted data used to make decisions about urban space – including automated decision-making with artificial intelligence and facial recognition technologies and the surveillance of urban space itself and the bodies that move through it.

The former tends to attract most attention and alarm in contemporary scholarship and popular media. Rapid advances in technology have intensified the reach and power of surveillance systems through the integration of surveillance technology into personal electronics, electronic banking and online purchasing, the ubiquity of QR codes, workplace and education tools (Greenspan, 2021; Kitchin, 2014). As Lyon notes (2018), surveillance of individual behaviour is created through consumer activity, both passively and actively, and as such we are willing participants in our own surveillance. Surveillance has become domesticated into workplaces, schools and transport, but also in homes (Mäkinen, 2016). This shifts the emphasis from surveillance being done 'to' ordinary people, citizens and non-citizens, to surveillance being done 'with' people. COVID-19 accelerated the enrolment of more and more people into surveillance systems as governments intensified ways to track, diagnose, notify and isolate individuals in real time (Isin & Ruppert, 2020; McDuie-Ra et al., 2024).

It is the latter – surveillance of space and the bodies that move through it, dwell in it, claim it, play with it – that is most relevant to counterinsurgency directed at play. The surveillance of space is ubiquitous in most urban environments (Klauser, 2013: 291). Surveillance of space includes basic techniques like walls and barriers to corral bodies into visible patches, to the human-to-human gaze of in situ surveillance at a checkpoint or entryway, to the human-to-screen-to-camera-to-human gaze of urban space filmed by CCTV, to higher-end technology through drones, facial recognition and integrated command and control rooms. Everyday urban life can be characterised by the 'mutual constitution and tensions' between 'fluidity and fixity, flows and presences, circulations and enclosures, external separation and internal organisation' (Klauser, 2013: 291).

Insurgent play activates counterinsurgent surveillance when claims on space are made. Crucially, bodies matter in the moment, not abstracted data and other algorithmic representations. And what bodies are *doing* in these spaces – insurgent acts such as playing, claiming, disrupting, wounding as described in Chapter 2 – activates existing surveillance systems, encourages the creation of new surveillance systems and drives play-seekers to spaces where surveillance is ineffective or absent. There may be some connection to surveillance systems tracking bodies at scale, such as all city control rooms (Luque-Ayala & Marvin, 2016), drones (Jensen, 2016) or specific urban zones monitored by live surveillance (Caprotti, 2019). However, generally insurgent play is countered by surveillance of small patches of the city: the street front outside a single building, a specific handrail or ledge, the roof of a car park.

Given the macro-relationships between race, surveillance and policing across much of the world, the racialised body doing the play matters acutely when it comes to surveillance of small spaces. As with other surveillance systems that seek to apprehend bodies in real time, race structures surveillance of insurgent play. Responses and consequences are more punitive and more rapid when 'blackness enters the frame' (Browne, 2015: 161). Race, thus, is a component of the variegated radical attunement discussed in Chapter 2, along with gender, sexuality, language, appearance, age, dis/ability. The relationships between race, insurgent play and surveillance are contextual. In skateboarding's heartlands in the urban United States, the United Kingdom and Europe, bodies of colour are quickly cast as suspicious by authorities and other citizens as part of 'affective taxonomies' that fuse 'racial anxiety' with notions of what actions are 'out of place' and 'inflammatory' (Ritchie, 2020: 15). Similar taxonomies hold in other vibrant skateboarding communities in Brazil, Colombia or South Africa, for example. Yet different dynamics to white/non-white shape surveillance responses to insurgent play in Japan, Singapore or Thailand, for example, all contexts discussed in this book. In these contexts, age (youth), class, dress, hairstyle, disposition, substance use (smoking, drinking), rather than obvious racial distinctions shape affective taxonomies of surveillance and intensify responses.

The interplay between insurgent play and counterinsurgent surveillance has rhythms. These rhythms are quickly learnt by skateboarders, like other urban insurgents, and by the humans charged with counterinsurgency, yet these rhythms are more difficult to perceive among onlookers. The most obvious surveillance tools are cameras. There is an extraordinary range of surveillance cameras scattered all over the built environment. Some date from the 1980s and 1990s and likely feed to a correspondingly old console and recording equipment. Cameras from the last 20 years might look 'all seeing' especially cameras encased in spherical semi-opaque casings, but they also have glitches – dead spots, odd angles, obstructions and limited visual fields. They rely upon human monitoring for live intervention, though they are effective at sorting surveillance footage for later use.

Cutting-edge surveillance that can capture fast-moving objects in high resolution is far more insidious (Narayan, 2023). Images can be analysed using facial recognition technology in real time, matching insurgent faces and bodies with previous data matches. In some jurisdictions, these matches can be used in broader counterinsurgent tactics despite the well-chronicled flaws and biases in existing facial recognition technology (Stevens & Keyes, 2021). Long-range surveillance equipment, using shortwave infrared spectrum technology for example, is more complicated because the existence of the equipment can't always be identified in the small patches of the city claimed for insurgent play. In other words, it is hard to see any cameras around, but the space may be under long-range surveillance. However, given the multiplicity of territorial forms for insurgent play, long-range surveillance is not yet a major factor in counterinsurgency against play.

The following figures come as sets of two, showing typical spaces disrupted by insurgent play and the surveillance tools in proximity (Figures 4.2 and 4.3; Figures 4.4 and 4.5).

Through repeated disruption, skateboarders develop attunement and ways to test surveillance systems. The first is to just skate, to play and wait. If no one comes, keep playing. Part of this technique is to play softly: a few pushes, a few tricks, nothing that damages surfaces, no modification or repair and just test the distance between 'controlled space' and the 'control space' (Klauser, 2017: 132). After a few visits, it's possible to gauge a rhythm of that distance. The time taken between starting play and intervention by property owners, security personnel or law enforcement is data for insurgents. This data is shared among other insurgents, low-key intelligence about a loading dock, a drainage ditch, a pedestrian plaza.

The second is to play hard, attempting a trick on the surfaces to maximise the time taken to bridge the distance between the controlled space and the control space. Rather than waiting to find out the rhythms of counterinsurgency, this approach directly challenges surveillance systems, demonstrating their futility in stopping disruption with intent. This approach is common in cities where surveillance is well-established, and the underlying assumption is that insurgent play will be challenged. So, the logic is to play hard until the inevitable kick-out.

One of the best ways to illustrate this is to consider insurgent play in Tokyo. Tokyo – like other famed insurgent play cities in Japan such as Kobe and Osaka – has a mixture of electronic and human surveillance of the urban landscape, often well synchronised with one another. In other words, the distance between controlled space and control space is short, measured in both space and time. Play at a spot and expect swift counterinsurgency. These rhythms are well understood by Tokyo skateboarders, and insurgent play is more common after dark, long after dark. As a consequence, it can be difficult to spot acts of insurgent play in daylight hours, but the marks left behind, the claims on space, are common in plain sight, as in Figure 4.6. Disruption after dark is a constant

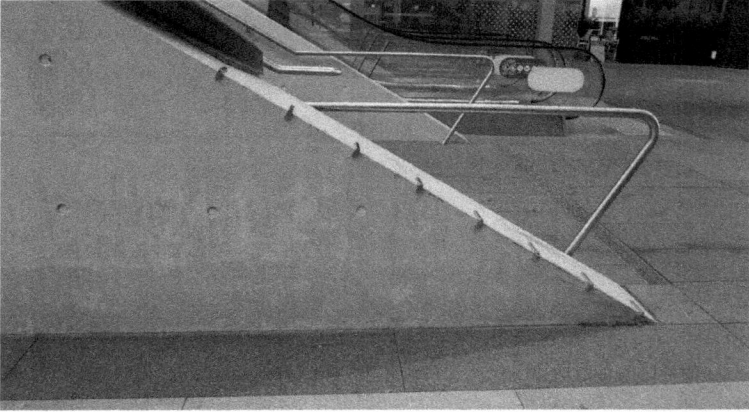

Figures 4.2 and 4.3 The angled ledge in Barangaroo, Sydney, is popular with skateboarders. In response, the surface has been covered with skatestoppers (4.2); the type here are 'nosings', and a surveillance camera captures the landing zone (4.3). Photos: McDuie-Ra.

in skateboard media from Japan, where filmers and photographers make use of streetlights, building lights, illuminated signs, flashes and portable LED (light-emitting diode) to produce kaleidoscopic clips and still images, with the variegated speed of bodies, boards and lights creating stunning archives of urban play. By contrast, in daylight there is no time to test the rhythms of surveillance. Skateboarders must make the most of the short window, minutes before a surveillance camera or passing pedestrian alerts the police or security guards stationed in and around commercial buildings. Short moments of disruption make territorial claims much more difficult, but repeated play, even in short bursts, can constitute claims. In *Animated Lands* (2020), discussed at length in Chapter 1, Brighenti and Kärrholm are generous with the temporalities and boundaries of territories. They adopt what they term a 'neovitalist' perspective to explore rhythm with 'reference to the intensive situations and moments it generates and, in the end, territorializes' (2020: 8). Even with responsive counterinsurgent surveillance, it is possible to make territorial claims through repeated moments of disruption.

The third approach is reconnaissance, reading the surfaces for evidence of play. Here, the focus shifts from the surveillance cameras and systems to evidence of other disruptions and territorial claims. For skateboarders, a telling giveaway are surfaces that have been repaired, modified and cared for using the techniques discussed in Chapter 3 or the marks and traces left by shredding. These tracings suggest the space has been used for play by others for long enough to wear down surfaces and activate repair techniques. The traces in Figure 4.7 are a good example. This spot, adjacent to the entrance

Figure 4.3 (Continued)

of the Kuala Lumpur Stock Exchange, is a no-go during the week. On closer inspection, the wheel marks on the vertical retaining wall and the wax marks on the edges of the stairs are signs that the spot is playable at other times, and play must happen often enough for the marks to remain through heat and heavy rain. There are other claims marked out in other ways on material space that suggest weak surveillance or disinterested actors in the control space: vandalism, debris, improvised shelter, graffiti, drug paraphernalia, ruderal growth, animal habitation. These spaces have been disrupted by other actors/actants and are subject to overlapping claims, overlapping insurgencies and as such suggest the possibilities of further disruption.

Spots entirely free of surveillance are almost always found where infrastructure is old, remote, underutilised or hidden from view. Un-surveilled spaces are open to modification by skaters; improving objects and surfaces for play, culminating in intricate DIY spaces incorporating existing infrastructure in vacant lots, underneath flyovers and bridges and in abandoned buildings, disrupting the existing order and positioning skaters as 'spatial activists' (Hollett & Vivoni, 2021: 13). There are scores of famous DIY spots built away from the 'techniques of attention' around the world, a phenomenon discussed in the following chapter.

Surveillance rhythms can change over longer periods of time too; a spot might have been free of surveillance for years but following improvements, an increase in value, a new tenant or a crackdown on insurgence by authorities, surveillance gets upgraded and the response to disruption speeds up. Surveillance keeps skateboarders moving through the urban landscape to new spaces, from spaces with swift surveillance to spaces with a longer lag between attention and intervention. The reverse is also true, in that spaces

Figures 4.4 and 4.5 The marble ledge in Singapore is perfect for play and surprisingly has no skatestoppers (most surfaces in the city do). However, it falls directly in view of the cluster of cameras shown in Figure 4.5. Photos: McDuie-Ra.

that were once surveilled become less important over time as urban flows bypass them, economic malaise sets in or the space falls into disrepair or ruin.

Skatestoppers

A standard skatestopper is a steel object that could fit in a human palm, partially sunken into the surface of a ledge, a bench or a handrail. Skatestoppers are an

Figure 4.5 (Continued)

essential part of low-tech counterinsurgency as a stand-in for – or extension of – human and electronic surveillance systems. In seeking to protect unauthorised movement across surfaces, skatestoppers highlight the tensions between 'fluidity and fixity, flows and presences, circulations and enclosures, external separation and internal organisation' (Klauser, 2013: 219), and of most relevance to insurgent play: disruption and order.

   Skatestoppers come in various shapes: spherical or cylindrical knobs, spikes and 'nosings', 'blades' and 'fins', strips affixed to both the vertical and horizontal edge of a ledge or covering the entire width of a flat surface. The

Figure 4.6 Traces in Tokyo. This angled wall displays marks from wheels, including skateboard wheels and bike wheels, plus handprints higher up where bodies would be steadied while wheels grip the wall, all in direct view of a surveillance camera and several signs advising of surveillance. Photo: McDuie-Ra.

aim is to interrupt surface flow with hard objects or 'folds' (Wylie, 2006), that stop movement, that stop play. To be effective, a series of skatestoppers will be installed across the length of a surface in neat rows, as in Figure 4.2 above and 4.8 below. Crucially, skatestoppers are installed *specifically* and *exclusively* to stop skateboarding. The presence of skatestoppers on surfaces, their absence, signs of their removal and signs of re-installation, record battles

Figure 4.7 Traces outside the Kuala Lumpur Stock Exchange. The angled embankment, stair edges and curved concrete wall assemble a complex play space in an area of high surveillance. Photo: McDuie-Ra.

between skateboarders and those trying to stop them, as well as larger battles over competing visions of the city, of order and of use.

Unlike more commonly analysed examples of counterinsurgency, skatestoppers are barely noticed outside the world of insurgent play despite their ubiquity in everyday urban life. Purpose-built skatestoppers originated in California in the late 1990s. Since then, skatestoppers have travelled to a

Figure 4.8 Blades, Tokyo. Photo: McDuie-Ra.

startling range of urban environments as street skateboarding has globalised. Skatestoppers are marketed as being on duty all the time, a cheap alternative to paying humans a salary and to investing in surveillance systems and their maintenance. In cities where human surveillance of spaces, buildings and precincts is common and constant, skatestoppers are less valuable as a counterinsurgent tactic. In these cities, or patches of these cities, authorities and property owners may opt for the 'clean' aesthetics of surfaces without skatestoppers, as in Figures 4.4 and 4.5 above from Singapore, and rely instead on other counterinsurgent tactics. Unlike skatestoppers, humans can be open to negotiation, and they also have shift changes and bathroom breaks. Skatestoppers remove any chance of kindness or irregular rhythm.

Skatestoppers promise three things. First, aesthetic order. A row of uniform stainless-steel objects protruding from different surfaces is more orderly than wax applied by skaters, grind marks and flecks of paint (see Chapter 3). A preference for aesthetic order is promoted by manufacturers as universal good. Second, social order. Skatestoppers promote the idea that urban space should be free of particular social groups with alternative ideas for use, including but not limited to play, and alternative aesthetic, somatic and material practices. These objects don't just protect the surfaces, they deter people from dwelling in the space entirely, ensuring only appropriate users dare pause. This sentiment goes beyond deterring play as a somatic act to deterring the presence of skateboarders and the prospect of free-for-alls. Third, anticipatory order. Skatestoppers are relatively inexpensive to install and are far cheaper than monitored surveillance systems and human wages. They are marketed as easy to install with limited expertise, especially prefabricated knobs and blades. In some cities, custom objects are installed to counter insurgent play that don't resemble the standard skatestopper, but have the same effects, such as the thick bars at an entry plaza in Singapore in Figure 4.9. Retrofitting is an option for surfaces once claimed for play. Yet there is a noticeable shift

Figure 4.9 Custom skatestoppers down the length of the angled ledge (or hubba) in Singapore. Photos: McDuie-Ra.

in the last decade to include skatestoppers in new buildings, infrastructure, vehicle and pedestrian throughways, common areas and outdoor furniture in the design phase. In other words, they are pre-installed in anticipation of insurgence and in anticipation of the future need for order, rather than after spaces and surfaces are subject to claims. As such, skatestoppers have shifted from reactionary to anticipatory, from stopping to deterring. As a result of this shift, the skatestopper has now become a standardised urban object in many cities *regardless* of whether the landscape draws skateboarders; new surfaces are born counterinsurgent.

In many cities, especially in the Global North, there is simultaneous investment in skatestoppers and in skateparks. The investment in skateparks can also be seen as a counterinsurgent strategy, to corral play into designated spaces, thereby reducing the potential for disruption in the rest of the city. Further, the existence of designated spaces justifies harsher counterinsurgent tactics elsewhere. As such, skatestoppers are increasing even as authorities appear much more open to forms of play like skateboarding, yet openness is only for orderly versions of play, in the correct spaces, on predetermined obstacles.

Challenging Counterinsurgency

There are two main ways that counterinsurgency is challenged: public activism and covert activism. Public activism to remove skate stoppers targets the government, usually municipal authorities or equivalent and is couched in larger arguments about space, use, legality and diversity. Public campaigns against skatestoppers have taken shape in different cities globally, including the South Bank undercroft in London (see Mould, 2015; Long Live Southbank, 2021; Warin, 2018), the Bentway in Toronto (Glover et al., 2022) or entire cities, such as Bordeaux, Malmö and Tampere (Book & Eden, 2021; Miaux & Garneau, 2016). The arguments in these campaigns use the rhetoric of city authorities around creativity, access and openness to make a case for liberating public space; questioning the value for money of skatestoppers; emphasising the vitality brought to city spaces by free play; and accentuating the value added to city 'brands'. Notably, these campaigns are overwhelmingly focused on public space. This focus stands to reason, as public space governed by public authorities is open to public activism. Yet not all, or even most, insurgent play takes place in clearly delineated public space, which will be discussed further below.

Led by professional skateboarder Leo Valls, the Play Project in Bordeaux is fascinating in that it focused on liberating existing spaces subject to counterinsurgent tactics and creating new skateable sculptures and public art to add to the city over a six-year period. In a 2020 interview, Valls recalls, 'we were trying to have a global vision for the city, to think about how people could skate from one spot to another and cruise around town, but also make sure skateboarding would blend well with the other uses of these public spaces' (Schwinghammer, 2020). Part of this process included removing skatestoppers and restoring the flow of existing surfaces. A further tactic was to add ordinary urban objects desired for play to parts of the city to bring vitality. Valls and his team proposed the city purchase 15 heavy granite benches (that can't be lifted and carried away but can be moved with heavy machinery) and had them placed in five different zones to 'activate' these spaces. Crucial to the design is the diffusion of spaces across the city and the refusal to corral skateboarding to a limited number of designated sites. The whole city is liberated. However, while the project has had the support of politicians, engagement with other urban dwellers is more complicated. Valls again,

> For the other city users it's still sometimes complicated. Even when we set up the sculptures some people would still complain that we fuck up pieces of art, even if it was made for skateboarding […] There is still a lot to communicate and explain. I think many citizens are still confused when they see a granite bench that is made for skateboarding but is also used to sit. They don't understand the concept. […] Skateboarding is a big part of our lives, it's a part of the city and they have to accept that. It's not always easy but in general it's good to talk to people. […] The whole point of a city and the furniture in it is, that it's for different users. But a lot of people just see the city as a place to work and consume. They get a little offended when we use the city too freely.

Bordeaux has become a liberated zone, free of counterinsurgency targeting play. The experience of the zone is tenuous though, reliant on political good-will, the value proposition for the city (branding) and the skill of well-organised activists. The scale of the city helps too; much of central Bordeaux has limited access for cars. These factors are difficult to align in many contexts, and it is unsurprising that successful public activism to liberate zones from counterinsurgency are all in small-sized European cities – Tampere, Malmö, Bordeaux.

In contrast, covert activism draws much less academic and public attention because it is difficult to couch in grander narratives. Mostly invisible to the unattuned, covert activism is rarely entangled in larger battles over urban space, philosophical debates on enclosure and commons and dialogue with politicians and the public. The best acts of liberation are small gestures, ideally undetectable, rather than grand gestures with the promise of alternative futures.

There is also a crucial temporal difference. Public activist campaigns such as the Play Project seek longevity through liberation, whereas covert activism is high risk; the liberated space may last a few days or a few years. Few skateboarders will take on the risk and cost of liberating a spot that won't function as play space or that might result in an increased crackdown on skateboarding in a particular area or neighbourhood. Direct liberation involves removing skate stoppers and, in some cases, patching up holes or chips in the surface material to restore the smooth flow. Sometimes only a few skatestoppers will be removed to allay attention on the deed for as long as possible.

Removing skatestoppers without damaging the surfaces is difficult. Some can be whacked off with a hammer without causing damage, though usually only if they are poorly installed or added retroactively to a damaged surface. Most skatestoppers are fastened with bonding agents and screws – some of which have unusual keys that make standard screwdrivers ineffective. There are tool kits available specifically designed for these bolts, and adept insurgents usually keep a set. Some skatestoppers are sunk deep into different surfaces and must be cut off using an electric grinder and other metal saws. Once loose, they can be knocked off with a hammer, though this can damage the surface, so care needs to be taken. On some surfaces, bolts and parts of the skatestopper cannot be removed, so they are ground down to the surface level; this can leave shards of metal poking out. Holes and missing chunks can be patched up using the repair techniques described in the previous chapter (Figure 4.10). Of course, spaces under surveillance make all these techniques riskier. As mentioned earlier in the chapter, race, class and other factors intensify risk for certain liberators. And the most effective covert activism takes place long after dark, with minimal noise and with neat repair work.

Conclusion

Cities are covered in hostile design objects targeting disruption, including insurgent play. Playing outside designated play space activates existing surveillance systems, encourages the creation of new surveillance systems and pushes insurgent players to appropriate space that is poorly surveilled. Surveillance systems exist in a wide range of forms and represent a vast time span of technologies, from closed-circuit television (CCTV) monitored live by humans to automated surveillance systems using facial recognition. Crucially, surveilling insurgent play focuses on bodies in the moment, not abstracted data. Skateboarders are attuned to the rhythms of surveillance

Figure 4.10 Liberated surface with ghostly imprint. If you look closely, the indent from the skatestopper has been filled with Bondo to restore the surface flow. Photos: McDuie-Ra.

systems and find ways to play in their glitches, constantly testing the distance, in space and in time, between the 'controlled space' and the 'control space' (Klauser, 2013). These systems have confederate relations with human act-ants, police, security guards, property owners who can intervene and restore order. Yet they don't always come. And through play, skateboarders create counterrhythms and in doing so make claims on space that approximate ter-ritorial claims, even if fleeting.

In contrast to the partially invisible networks of surveillance are the ubiquitous skatestoppers covering the surfaces of cities globally, though with a
higher concentration in the Global North where in situ human surveillance is
waning. These steel objects, partially sunken into the surfaces of the city, epit-
omise attempts to reinstate order while introducing obnoxious objects that
suck the life out of urban space for everyone. Skatestoppers and related hostile
design elements seem trivial when considered against armed humans, weap-
ons, machines, walls and barricades and ubiquitous surveillance with automated systems using facial recognition and other sorting tools. However, they
are related. As Kurt Iveson (2010) writes in the case of graffiti and military
urbanism, there is a pervasive logic among authorities that graffiti writers
– fellow insurgents – exploit the same vulnerabilities as crime gangs and ter-
rorists. Skatestoppers stop play and therefore stop unpredictable movement,
unpredictable noise and unsanctioned visual disruption, draining spaces
of their vitality, leaving them empty, functional and orderly. Writing about
counterinsurgency historically, Achille Mbembe argues that its tactics 'create
a partition in time and an atomization of space' (2017: 4) turning everyday
space into 'battlespace' (Graham, 2009). Through public and covert activism,
insurgents and their allies take on the atomisation of urban space by removing counterinsurgent objects, creating zones for play outside the rules and
laws governing space. These liberated zones might be temporary, but that is
all insurgent players need to create moments of joy amidst enclosure.

Chapter 5

UNDER THE FLYOVER

Shannon Mattern argues that cities are not just sites of information access (and production) but a medium themselves. She writes, 'our physical landscapes inscribe, transmit, and even embody information – about their histories, their state of repair, their potential uses, and so forth' (2017: xii). In this vein, insurgent play inscribes new uses, unintended uses, covert uses. In this concluding chapter, I want to close with an account of the zenith of insurgent play, the spaces underneath flyovers. Flyovers are cast, and demanded, as a solution to density. Whether coveted or reviled, all flyovers have an underside. The underside of flyovers provides obscured patches for insurgent play. Concrete pillars, angled drains, supporting walls can all be utilised to make insurgent play space, along with fabricated ramps, bumps and pilfered street objects. The meshwork of built forms, waste, plants, animals and weather shape and reshape the underside of flyovers in ways unlike more visible spaces because the underside is the afterthought of elevated vehicular mobility. The underside is also the dark side, a space for the nefarious, the antisocial, the outcast. Rarely are these leftover spaces explored as play space. Yet globally, the best place to find insurgent play space is under a flyover. Seriously. Go and see.

I propose the spaces created under flyovers as an alternative to the open public space coveted in SDG 11, discussed in Chapter 1. The underside of flyovers is the insurgent parkland, the insurgent pitch or court, the insurgent playground. In some cities, the underside of flyovers is turned into open public space for free use and/or designated use. However, in much of the world, the underside of flyovers is leftover space. Leftover space is used to build shelter, to peddle goods, to dump waste, to park vehicles and to play. Given the ubiquity of the flyover as global urban form, undersides have the potential to be universal insurgent play spaces especially when fabricated using DIY techniques described in Chapter 3.

DIY skate spots are user-created play space for skateboarding and other expressions of play. As Glenney and O'Connor write (2019: 846),

DIY spaces are extensions of home-life; it is common to see open drinking, fires, BBQs, bands and even sleeping. In addition, unlike skateparks, DIY skateboarding is firmly accepted in skateboard films and magazines. Hence, these are not city spaces – spaces informed by city-planning and design – but rather urban spaces informed by the planning and design of the citizens, and thereby used more readily by them.

The best DIY play spaces are located away from residential areas, active commercial spaces and valuable real estate where the built environment can be remade and fabrication of new objects for play is possible. Successful fabrication depends on minimal surveillance, ease of trespass, including with cement and other building materials and with some kind of sonic barriers; fabrication is very loud. DIY spaces demonstrate the desire (Chapter 2), maintenance and fabrication (Chapter 3) and the measures taken to avoid counterinsurgency (Chapter 4). They are the firmest territorial claims made for insurgent play. They involve hundreds of hours of labour, maintenance and thrive when their location is kept quiet. And the best spaces to make claimclaims and escape attention are the city's undersides.

Flyovers Everywhere

I use the term 'flyover' to refer to elevated infrastructure for cars, public transit and pedestrians. I recognise that this is not the perfect or even an accurate term.[1] However, flyover resonates because the name suggests there is an underside to the 'over'. Flyovers aren't just created for cars; elevated pedestrian and cycle paths, mass transit systems, cable cars are similarly intended to solve mobility bottlenecks and, in some cases, demonstrate progress, modernity and even 'world-class urbanism' (Lederman, 2020). In *Modern Mobility Aloft* (2020), Amy Finstein examines elevated highway planning, construction and degradation (and collapse) in Chicago, New York and Boston at the turn of the twentieth century. As American cities grew vertically, 'design dialogues increasingly focused on developing a specific architectural language specific to the skyscraper form' and 'ultimately cast elevated highways as critical components in redesigning the organization,

---

1 When it comes to automotive infrastructure, 'freeway' or 'expressway' are commonly used regardless of whether the road is elevated. Elevated public transit infrastructure is often referred to by its local name, often an acronym, such as the MTR in Hong Kong, MRT in Singapore or BTS Skytrain in Bangkok. Elevated pedestrian infrastructure can be referred to as a bridge, an overpass, linkways, crosswalks and so on.

efficiency, and appearance of modern cities' (2020: 27). Elevated highways to separate traffic vertically were viewed by all stakeholders as 'central features of their futuristic visions' (2020: 3). Finstein adds, elevated highways were seen as 'threads of modern travel and communication woven into the very fabric of new urban landscapes' (2020: 216). And despite collapse, demolition and repurposing in some cities (see Mohl, 2012), the association of the elevated highway with modern urban landscapes and futurity has travelled with the form to different parts of the world.

Flyovers materialise verticality, but they are also allies of sprawl. In *Sprawltown*, Richard Ingersoll writes, 'once understood as something that occurred on the city's edge, sprawl can now be found between cities and even within the historic district of a city', from sprawling cities in the United States (where many of Ingersoll's examples are drawn) to cities like Cairo and Lima (2006: 3–4). Flyovers encourage sprawl by giving commuters the opportunity to 'fly' over intermediary areas – residential, industrial, commercial, agricultural, 'natural' – to reach desired destinations. For Ingersoll, the 'complex weave' of elevated highways and flyovers are the 'cathedrals of mobility', that 'incite a painful beauty' (2006: 101). Ingersoll extols flyovers, which he refers to variously as 'aerial highways' and 'elevated highway interchanges'. Yet Ingersoll's awe, his invocation of the sublime, is tainted by the consumption these cathedrals introduce into everyday life. A photograph of a Shanghai flyover is captioned by Ingersoll as a 'frightening beauty' (2006: 102).

In *Infrastructure: A Guide to the Industrial Landscape*, Brian Hayes suggests that a major factor in elevated roadways are crossroads (2005/2014). Grade-separated intersections take traffic onto overpasses and underpasses; however, it is the 'on' and 'off' ramps that create the need for more flyovers, often curved. Hayes identifies three main forms: the diamond, the cloverleaf and the elaborate directional interchange, the 'brute-force solution' (2005/2014: 355). In the directional interchange (or stack interchange), the 'ramps do the weaving, rather than the drivers' (2005/2014: 355). The curvature of the ramps is mild, meaning vehicles can turn in any direction without stopping or even slowing down, accentuating flow and efficiency. The problem is, as Hayes puts it, 'even the overpasses and underpasses have overpasses and underpasses' (2005/2014: 355). And while 'the concrete confection is visually very impressive from the air', they are expensive, ecologically hazardous and take up enormous tracts of land (2005/2014: 355).

Famous examples include the four-layered, 22-lane 'Stack' in Los Angeles, connecting the 101 and 110 freeways, opened in 1953. Arthur Krim argues that 'the "Stack" symbolized the dominance of the freeway and automobile mobility in the suburban growth of Los Angeles' and, as portrayed in national print media, 'became the singular symbol of the city' by the late 1950s (1992:

125). Critique gave way to appreciation, even desire. Stack aesthetics are a constant in literature, film, television and other media forms (Deleyto, 2017; López-Calvo, 2011; Murphet, 2001). Stephen Graham (2018) argues that flyovers are an integral part of elite visions of world-class urbanism in the Global South. For Graham, these 'ubiquitous strips of raised asphalt and concrete' have been neglected in critical urban research in favour of more spectacular sites, such as airports, infrastructure for mega events, technology parks and skylines (2018: 527–8). In Asia, flyovers are popular amidst spectacular urban growth, vertically and as sprawl (Jenks, 2003; Kennedy & Sood, 2016; Nethercote, 2018). Verticality takes hold in mega-cities (Burte, 2024), in planned, formal settlements, and in unplanned, informal settlements (Zugayar et al., 2021). Building up, rather than out, veers urban development away from contentious politics around land, displacement and resettlement, at least in theory (Shih & Chiang, 2022). In practice, verticality and sprawl are co-constitutive, and connective infrastructure such as public transport, highways and flyovers spread 'out' even as cities grow 'up' (and 'down').

While the flyover may have been pioneered in North America, the spread of the form in the Global South evokes Asia and China in particular. Miraculous urban growth is materialised in Chinese cities like Shenzhen (Guangdong Province), shifting the locus of flyover power and popularity away from North America. Shenzhen began the experiment of opening China after being founded as a Special Economic Zone (SEZ) in 1980, and as each enclave of the city developed, a citywide transportation network called 'seven horizontal and thirteen vertical' freeways and overpasses was built (Huang, 2017: 73). And this model has spread far, including to countries in Africa, such as Kenya. Here, 'plug-in urbanism', what Guma et al. call 'go-to projects that come complete from elsewhere, designed and conceived as obvious solutions to identified problems' (2023: 2551), dominates urban development. Guma et al. use the example of the Nairobi Expressway, a project that 'inherits and imitates foreign policy models, technological machinery and architectural styles and designs from China' (2023: 2559).

The counterpoint to awe is doom; that flyovers create more problems than they solve. Often attributed to the desires of 'elites', as either/both a planning elite or elite constituents as the key beneficiaries, doomed flyover construction is invoked where urban development is marked by stark social and economic divisions (Roy, 2011). For Graham, flyover construction always 'involves powerful struggles over the politics of who's movement matters, and who can be systematically constrained or interrupted' (2018: 534). This is pronounced in conflict-affected urban environments, such as Palestine and Cape Town, which he explores. The promise of flying over congestion, poverty, dust, mud and slower mobilities – from cycle- to animal-powered – is a powerful draw in cities like Mumbai, gravid with the promise of world-class urbanism for many of its residents (Burte, 2024). The prevalence of corruption and ineptitude intensifies the sense of doom, manifesting in flyovers promised and not delivered, or delivered only after years and years of waiting, or delivered of such poor quality that they create new bottlenecks, or that fall down and kill people.

Graham's argument about flyovers as elite instruments is convincing, suggesting each individual flyover is miraculous for a small few, doomed for everyone else. Yet beyond their function, dysfunction and beyond their violence, they remain objects of appreciation, even desire. Graham identifies this as a temporal lapse, with the Global South in the present failing to heed lessons from the Global North in the past and thus sowing destruction in their future. He writes, '[w]hat is striking, rather, is how the current fetish of the raised highway in Global South cities […] mirrors a similar preoccupation that gripped Europe and North America in the 1960s and 1970s' (2018: 530).

Though this critique seems too easy, support for flyovers is not reducible to an elite or even upper-middle-class sensibility. Flyovers and other infrastructure that promise to accelerate mobility can be exceptionally popular among non-elites too: motorcyclists, autorickshaw drivers, taxi and ride-share drivers or car owners. For instance, in some cities, such as Lahore in Pakistan, flyovers are reserved for – or give priority to – buses. Indeed, elites and upper-middle-class perspectives on flyovers and urban infrastructure lean closer to disappointment. As Heslop and Murton remind us, as new roads and transportation networks take shape, the experiences are uneven and unexpected. They write (2021: 23),

> Whether journeys become shorter, faster, more treacherous, cheaper, or more costly, questions about ownership, management, access to 'public goods', responsibility, and other critical concerns consistently take new shape.

Research on the 'broken promises' of cars (Hagman, 2006) and the general shift away from the primacy of the (private) automobile (Dowling & Simpson, 2013) often focus on Europe, the United States and Australia, bypassing the surge in car ownership in other parts of the world and the furious investment in infrastructure to match. Entangled in this infrastructure is the promise of cars (yet unbroken) for aspiring citizens for whom personal mobility appeals for obvious reasons of status, convenience and being free of contacts and encounters with other urban dwellers. More sprawl, more verticality, more cars, more flyovers. Countless flyovers mean countless undersides, countless potential play spaces.

Darkside, Underside, Playside

RK69 in Bangkok is a prototypical insurgent play space, and it allows us to explore some basic attributes of the interplay of flyovers and their undersides, their darksides, as play space. RK69 is built on space that has been found and claimed, not given and sanctioned. RK69 is built on disused outdoor basketball courts in Prawet, eastern Bangkok. The lot is surrounded by auto-body shops, used-car yards, garment wholesalers and warehouses, bounded to the north by the Phra Khanong River and the south by the busy On Nut-Phatthanakan junction, where multiple-lane highways cross over in a series of flyovers and elevated access ramps. One of these sections of flyover is built over the lot, curving from one corner of the rectangular space along the length of the lot (Figure 5.1). The thick concrete pillars supporting the flyover have become part of the DIY (Figure 5.2). The flyover is an essential ally in the insurgent play claims made here. Without it, the play space would not be hidden visually or buffered sonically from the surrounding city. The form of the flyover also creates objects to 'add-on' for play through fabrication.

The creators of RK69 fabricate an ever-changing play space to their tastes and style. Fabrication gives a sense of permanence, a strong base for a territorial claim when compared to fleeting uses, fleeting traces. The rhythms of play, construction and social bonds create belonging and exclusion, while 'animating' found space as territory (Brighenti & Kärrholm, 2020: 4). Some obstacles resemble the kinds of obstacles found in skateparks – quarter pipes, pool walls, ramp-to-walls, while others approximate street objects desired by skateboarders – curbs, ledges, embankments. Some of these obstacles are well-finished, suggesting confidence in longevity, despite there being no guarantee they will last. The section mimicking the wall of a pool has rows of

Figure 5.1 RK69 looking north to the Phra Khanong River. Photo: McDuie-Ra.

Figure 5.2 The pillars of the flyover used as play space and art space, RK 69. Note the fabrication around the pillar base. Photo: McDuie-Ra

small tiles near the coping (the rounded edge that skateboarders use to grind the surface – Figure 5.3). Other obstacles reveal their inner matter: chunks of broken brick, concrete and stones backed with cinder blocks and smoothed over with hand-trowelled cement. Lighting poles from the basketball court are still in place, though worn-out sneakers have been hurled up and suspended by their shoelaces, another territorial claim (Figure 5.4).

Graffiti covers the walls that divide the lot from the highway on its western side, on some of the angled surfaces, on patches of the ground, the vertical

Figure 5.3 Pool-style tiles, RK69. Photo: McDuie-Ra.

surfaces of the flyover pillars and on the equipment shed used to store building materials and a barbecue. Hazards abound. There are cracks in the different sections of ground surface from the heat and rain. Repair and care work discussed in Chapter 3 fall to the users and custodians of the space. There are bottles, cigarette butts, pill blister packs, rebar, stones, sacks, puddles and a few wayward plants. There are brooms for sweeping up debris, squeegees for mopping up water and plastic buckets for mixing cement and synthetic filler. The location is well hidden by the infrastructure entrapping it, making

Figure 5.4 Shoes tossed over the lighting rig, RK69. Photo: McDuie-Ra.

hours of community labour to produce and maintain the space with minimal outside interference.

Despite its illegality, RK69 is not hidden. The spot is featured in videos and photos posted on social media of barbecues, bands playing and skateboarding by skaters ranging from professional to beginner, middle-aged to children. RK69 has had a social media account on various platforms, some active and some now defunct. RK69 was featured in *Confusion* skate magazine in 2020 with an accompanying video (Venter, 2020). RK69 is commonly featured in video 'guides' to Bangkok's skateboarding scene posted on video-sharing platforms, all easily discoverable. The spot is 'pinned' on most of the main digital mapping platforms (e.g. you can search for it on Google Maps). The 'edgy' aesthetic draws people from outside the subculture too. On one of my trips to RK69, a photographer, lighting technician, makeup artist and fashion model climbed in through the hole in the fence. The model posed against the concrete and graffiti, going back through the fence and into the car to change into new outfits.

Despite this episode, RK69 is not subject to overtures from government or private capital, yet. It maintains an alternate rhythm, a disruptive rhythm, its own vitality.

Outro

Insurgent play happens anywhere. If, as play scholars argue, play is intrinsic to the human condition, then it can't wait. Play can't wait for the appropriate space to be built, for surveillance of existing spaces to be muted, for designated uses to be loosened (see Franck & Stevens, 2006). Planners and governments are fond of imagining play space, particularly in multi-use, open public space; the zenith of good urban planning and the breeding ground for creativity. While such planning orthodoxy is widespread, politically and geographically, data suggests that the existence of open public space, and the play space nested within it, is woefully inadequate in towns and cities globally (see Chapter 1). Crucially, even where open space *does* exist, the 'openness' can be limited. In the rare cities where there is an abundance of open, accessible, free public space, including space for play, insurgent play still happens. The coexistence of designated play space and insurgent play space baffles authorities and planners. Why, when spaces are made for play, do people play elsewhere? Why when the needs for play are met by fixed spaces, fixed objects and carefully chosen surfaces, do humans seek fluid spaces, alter objects and transform surfaces? Simply, disruption is playful, fun, expressive, addictive and arguably, instincitve.

In this book, I have argued that insurgent play is generated from both an absence of play space and the desire to disrupt. Thus, adding more play space doesn't remove the impetus for insurgence. Insurgent play continues because it fulfils the desire for play without prescription, without designation, without containment, without surveillance. Though insurgence begets surveillance, as discussed in Chapter 4, and surveillance is attuned to various racialised, gendered and class dynamics in different contexts. Insurgent play flows from the desire for disruption, whether a disruption of rules, of design intentions, of order – understood as both the order of the material landscapes and the order reproduced by bodies in spaces and on the move between them. As such, insurgent play is bodily expression that challenges, disrupts and transgresses dominant ways of city-making and city-inhabiting. Insurgent play is counterpolitical play, play that challenges access and denial of access, amenities and their absence, property rights, surveillance, fences, walls, immobility and the imposition of order.

While the urban frontstage – the plazas, squares, waterfronts, pedestrian precincts – are obvious sites for insurgent play, to truly understand insurgent play is to pay attention to parts of the city we might not otherwise go, parts of the city we might not otherwise notice and parts of the city we might not otherwise consider as places for joy, expression and experimentation in urban living. In turn, we can expand on the methods we use to study counter politics and the acts, agents and markings that constitute these claims.

These claims aren't simply about who occupies space, why and for how long. The quality of that occupation, even if fleeting, enlivens the city. What bodies do in space matters for territorial claims. Insurgent play is expression, but movement is not constant. There are social worlds to insurgent play that move at different speeds, that repair and care for the surfaces and objects of

Figure 5.5 'JC' using the form of the backstage for play. Play brings this patch of the city to life in the hours it is otherwise dormant. Photo: L. O'Donnell, used with permission.

play space, that loiter and socialise. In this way, insurgent play disrupts and challenges urban orders while also generating communities and identities, (sub)cultures and art.

Insurgent play space is generated from below. It cannot be designed, though good design helps, and the smoother the surfaces of the city, the greater the play space. Though the reverse is also true, as in Chapter 4, objects that interrupt surface flow are the standard counterinsurgency tactic for impeding play. Insurgent play shapes identities that counter prevailing urban orders, their antecedents, and their remnants. And insurgent sensibilities, insurgent attunement to urban space, cannot be appeased by better urban planning. Nor will multiplying designated play spaces, creative precincts, and 'flexible' public spaces sate the desire for disruption. More designated play spaces are welcome in cities globally. The more, the better. The point here is that more designated play space will not quell the desire to disrupt the city through play, just as the preponderance of legal 'street art' and mural walls in cities globally has not curbed graffiti on other walls (Andron, 2018; Young, 2013).

Skateboarding is one form of insurgent play, and I have used it throughout this book for several reasons. First, street skateboarding happens in spaces designed for other uses, in new spaces of urban growth and renewal, spaces assembled over time with limited planning or design, and spaces marked by decline and abandonment. Skateboarding follows form, surface, smoothness, obstacles. In other words, it happens almost anywhere where surfaces of the city allow for urethane wheels to roll. This makes it possible, and observable, in a vast range of spaces globally. And, because skateboarding is mediated – in skateboarding media but also on the phones, cameras, and social media accounts of skateboarders at all levels – moments of insurgent play are captured and circulated in a constant network of image and sound; all of which depends upon making claims on spaces intended for other things. These claims are territorial and become part of an alternative system of knowledge, an alternative mapping, of cities based on insurgent play space.

Second, disruption of the city through somatic acts is the essence of playful expression in street skateboarding. Beyond this, disruption constitutes the fabric of social worlds that span divides of age, race, class and gender unevenly and imperfectly but in ways that are uncommon in most other urban spaces. To be clear, public and quasi-public spaces such as shopping malls, parks, beaches, mix everyone together. But rarely do they engage with one another, rarely do they share worlds. Skateboarding, like other high-risk insurgent play, bonds people though disruption.

Third, skateboarding leaves traces on the surfaces and objects of the city. These traces mark territory, allowing observers to see the outlines, the boundaries of territorial claims even when bodies are absent, when play is paused. It is not unique in this way, but compared to insurgent play that leaves almost no trace – dancing, martial arts, mass exercise – skateboarding draws confrontations, crackdowns, and counterinsurgency. In this way, skateboarding is a thick kind of insurgent play, living at the contentious end of the spectrum of claims made on space through play.

Finally, skateboarding is constantly being tamed by authorities, by planners, by corporate interests. Yet at the subcultural core of skateboarding is insurgence. Aspects of the subculture get parcelled into controlled spaces, profit-making representations and symbolic capital for tying creativity to place. Yet skateboarding continues to grow as insurgent play. The desire for certain forms, for damage, for wounding, the cultures of repair and care, and the counterinsurgent responses are global.

There are so many other kinds of play that take place outside designated play spaces, that disrupt the urban order, that bring life, vitality, to otherwise mundane patches of the city. In other words, there are multiple social worlds of disruption around play. My hope with this book is that the concept of insurgent play is used to talk about these worlds. As a concept, it gives us some rudimentary tools to think about what bodies do in space when they make counterclaims on access, use, custodianship and ownership. Furthermore, the paradigmatic ideas in SDG 11, that humans need open public space to live a decent urban life, are immensely valuable. As a normative agenda for the urban future, it is essential. However, play doesn't wait for open public space to be created. Play happens anywhere, everywhere, all the time. And insurgent play offers an alternative reading of where and when play happens.

BIBLIOGRAPHY

Abulhawa, D., 2020. *Skateboarding and Femininity: Gender, Space-making and Expressive Movement*. London: Routledge.

Alić, D., 2016. From Commemoration to Protest. In J. O'Callaghan, P. Hogben and R. Freestone (eds), *Sydney's Martin Place: A Cultural and Design History*. Crow's Nest: Allen and Unwin, pp. 475–501.

Amin, A., 2013. Telescopic urbanism and the poor. *City, 17*(4), pp. 476–492.

Amin, A., 2014. Lively infrastructure. *Theory, Culture & Society, 31*(7–8), pp. 137–161.

Anand, N., 2017. *Hydraulic City: Water and the Infrastructures of Citizenship in Mumbai*. Durham, NC: Duke University Press.

Andron, S., 2018. Selling streetness as experience: The role of street art tours in branding the creative city. *The Sociological Review, 66*(5), pp. 1036–1057.

Anguelovski, I., Connolly, J. and Brand, A.L., 2018. From landscapes of utopia to the margins of the green urban life: For whom is the new green city?. *City, 22*(3), pp. 417–436.

Arefin, M.R., 2019. Infrastructural discontent in the sanitary city: Waste, revolt, and repression in Cairo. *Antipode, 51*(4), pp. 1057–1078.

Arjmand, R., 2016. *Public Urban Space, Gender and Segregation: Women-only Urban Parks in Iran*. London: Routledge.

Ash, J. and Gallacher, L.A., 2011. Cultural geography and videogames. *Geography Compass, 5*(6), pp. 351–368.

Ashtari, D. and de Lange, M., 2019. Playful civic skills: A transdisciplinary approach to analyse participatory civic games. *Cities, 89*: 70–79.

Atencio, M., Beal, B. and Yochim, E.C., 2013. "It ain't just Black kids and white kids": The representation and reproduction of authentic "skurban" masculinities. *Sociology of Sport Journal, 30*(2), pp. 153–172.

Bächtold, S., 2023. Blackouts, whitelists, and 'terrorist others': The role of socio-technical imaginaries in Myanmar. *Journal of Intervention and Statebuilding, 17*(4), pp. 394–414.

Bäckström, Å. and Blackman, S., 2022. Skateboarding: From urban spaces to subcultural Olympians. *Young, 30*(2), pp. 121–131.

Badami, N., 2018. Informality as Fix: Repurposing jugaad in the post-crisis economy. *Third Text, 32*(1), pp. 46–54.

Baptista, I., 2019. Electricity services always in the making: Informality and the work of infrastructure maintenance and repair in an African city. *Urban Studies, 56*(3), pp. 510–525.

Barua, M., 2023. *Lively Cities: Reconfiguring Urban Ecology*. Minneapolis, MN: University of Minnesota Press.

Bateson, P. and Martin, P., 2013. *Play, Playfulness, Creativity, and Innovation.* Cambridge: Cambridge University Press.

Baumann, H., 2019. Disrupting movements, synchronising schedules: Time as an infrastructure of control in East Jerusalem. *City, 23*(4–5), pp. 589–605.

Bereitschaft, B., 2016. Gods of the city? Reflecting on city building games as an early introduction to urban systems. *Journal of Geography, 115*(2), pp. 51–60.

Bogle, M., 2016. Corridor of power. In J. O'Callaghan, P. Hogben, and R. Freestone (eds), *Sydney's Martin Place: A Cultural and Design History.* Crow's Nest: Allen and Unwin, pp. 171–210.

Book, K. and Svanborg Eden, G., 2021. Malmö–the skateboarding city: A multi-level approach for developing and marketing a city through user-driven partnerships. *International Journal of Sports Marketing and Sponsorship, 22*(1), pp. 164–178.

Borden, I., 2001. *Skateboarding, Space and the City: Architecture and the Body.* London: Berg.

Bos, D., 2023. Playful encounters: Games for geopolitical change. *Geopolitics, 28*(3), pp. 1210–1234.

Bou Akar, H., 2018. *For the War Yet to Come: Planning Beirut's Frontiers.* Palo Alto, CA: Stanford University Press.

Braier, M. and Yacobi, H., 2017. The planned, the unplanned and the hyper-planned: Dwelling in contemporary Jerusalem. *Planning Theory & Practice, 18*(1), pp. 109–124.

Brakke, G., 2023. Ambivalent insurgencies: Citizenship, land politics and development in Hanoi and its periurban fringe. *Urban Studies, 60*(6), pp. 1123–1138.

Brighenti, A.M. and Karrholm, M., 2020. *Animated Lands: Studies in Territoriology.* Lincoln, NE: University of Nebraska Press.

Browne, S., 2015. *Dark Matters: On the Surveillance of Blackness.* Durham, NC: Duke University Press.

Bryson, J.R., Billing, C. and Tewdwr-Jones, M., 2023. Urban infrastructure patching: Citizen-led solutions to infrastructure ruptures. *Urban Studies, 60*(10), pp. 1932–1948.

Burte, H., 2024. Mumbai's differential verticalisation: The dialectic of sovereign and technical planning rationalities. *Urban Studies, 61*(4), pp. 706–725.

Caprotti, F., 2019. Spaces of visibility in the smart city: Flagship urban spaces and the smart urban imaginary. *Urban Studies, 56*(12), pp. 2465–2479.

Carducci, V., 2006. Culture jamming: A sociological perspective. *Journal of Consumer Culture, 6*(1), pp. 116–138.

Carr, J.N., 2017. Skateboarding in dude space: The roles of space and sport in constructing gender among adult skateboarders. *Sociology of Sport Journal, 34*(1), pp. 25–34.

Castro, A. [Dir.], 2018. The Evolution of NYC's Black Hubba. *Jenkem Magazine.* Available at: https://www.jenkemmag.com/home/2018/07/09/the-evolution-of-the-nyc-black -hubba/. Accessed 3 July, 2021.

Castrucci, J. [Dir.], 2000. *Photosynthesis.* Alien Workshop. VHS.

Cervi, L. and Divon, T., 2023. Playful activism: Memetic performances of Palestinian resistance in TikTok# Challenges. *Social Media+ Society, 9*(1), p. 20563051231157607.

Chang, A.Y., 2019. *Playing Nature: Ecology in Video Games.* Minneapolis, MN: University of Minnesota Press.

Chang, T.C. and Mah, O.B., 2021. Beyond child's play: Heritage as process in Singapore's playgrounds. *International Journal of Heritage Studies, 27*(5), pp. 500–516.

Chiu, C. and Giamarino, C., 2019. Creativity, conviviality, and civil society in neoliberalizing public space: Changing politics and discourses in skateboarder activism from New York City to Los Angeles. *Journal of Sport and Social Issues, 43*(6), pp. 462–492.

Chiu, C., 2009. Contestation and conformity: Street and park skateboarding in New York City public space. *Space and Culture, 12*(1), pp. 25–42.

Corwin, J.E. and Gidwani, V., 2021. Repair work as care: On maintaining the planet in the Capitalocene. *Antipode*. https://doi.org/10.1111/anti.12791

Currans, E., 2017. *Marching Dykes, Liberated Sluts, and Concerned Mothers: Women Transforming Public Space*. Urbana, IL: University of Illinois Press.

D'Arcy, S., 2016. Temples of commerce. In J. O'Callaghan, P. Hogben, and R. Freestone (eds), *Sydney's Martin Place: A Cultural and Design History*. Crow's Nest: Allen and Unwin, pp. 212–248.

Davis, M., 1990. *City of Quartz: Excavating the Future in Los Angeles*. New York: Verso.

De Arce, R.P., 2018. *City of Play: An Architectural and Urban History of Recreation and Leisure*. London: Bloomsbury.

Degani, M., 2022. *The City Electric*. Durham, NC; Duke University Press.

Deleyto, C., 2017. *From Tinseltown to Bordertown: Los Angeles on Film*. Detroit, MI: Wayne State University Press.

Denham, J. and Spokes, M., 2021. The right to the virtual city: Rural retreatism in open-world video games. *New Media & Society, 23*(6), pp. 1567–1583.

Dinces, S., 2011. 'Flexible opposition': Skateboarding subcultures under the rubric of late capitalism. *The International Journal of the History of Sport, 28*(11), pp. 1512–1535.

Douglas, G.C., 2018. *The Help-Yourself City: Legitimacy and Inequality in DIY Urbanism*. Oxford: Oxford University Press.

Dovey, K., 2012. Informal urbanism and complex adaptive assemblage. *International Development Planning Review, 34*(4), pp. 349–368.

Dowling, R. and Simpson, C., 2013. 'Shift–the way you move': Reconstituting automobility. *Continuum, 27*(3), pp. 421–433.

Elden, S., 2013. Secure the volume: Vertical geopolitics and the depth of power. *Political Geography, 34*, pp. 35–51.

Felker-Kantor, M., 2018. *Policing Los Angeles: Race, Resistance, and the Rise of the LAPD*. Chapel Hill, NC: UNC Press Books.

Finstein, A., 2020. *Modern Mobility Aloft: Elevated Highways, Architecture, and Urban Change in Pre-Interstate America*. Philadelphia, PA: Temple University Press.

Fok, C.Y.L. and O'Connor, P., 2021. Chinese women skateboarders in Hong Kong: A skatefeminism approach. *International Review for the Sociology of Sport, 56*(3), pp. 399–415.

Forsyth, I., Lorimer, H., Merriman, P. and Robinson, J., 2013. What are surfaces?. *Environment and Planning A, 45*(5), pp. 1013–1020.

Fraile-Jurado, P., 2024. Geographical aspects of open-world video games. *Games and Culture, 19*(7), pp. 872–896.

Franck, K.A. and Stevens, Q., 2006. Tying down loose space. In K.A. Franck and Q. Stevens (ed.), *Loose space*. London: Routledge, pp. 1–33.

García-Lamarca, M., 2017. From occupying plazas to recuperating housing: Insurgent practices in Spain. *International Journal of Urban and Regional Research, 41*(1), pp. 37–53.

Geckle, B. and Shaw, S., 2022. Failure and futurity: The transformative potential of queer skateboarding. *Young, 30*(2), pp. 132–148.

Gelder, K., 2005. Introduction: The field of subcultural studies. In K. Gelber (ed.), *The Subcultures Reader*, 2nd Edition. Abingdon: Routledge, pp. 1–18.

Glenney, B., 2023. Polluted leisure enskilment: Skateboarding as ecosophy. *Leisure Sciences*, *46*(8), 1–25.

Glenney, B. and O'Connor, P., 2019. Skateparks as hybrid elements of the city. *Journal of Urban Design*, *24*(6), pp. 840–855.

Glenney, B. and O'Connor, P., 2023. Skateboarding as discordant: A rhythmanalysis of disaster leisure. *Sport, Ethics and Philosophy*, *17*(2), pp. 172–184.

Glover, T.D., Munro, S., Men, I., Loates, W. and Altman, I., 2022. Skateboarding, gentle activism, and the animation of public space: CITE–a celebration of skateboard arts and culture at the Bentway. In I.R. Lamond, Brett Lashua and Chelsea Reid (eds), *Leisure, Activism, and the Animation of the Urban Environment*, 1st Edition. London and New York: Routledge, pp. 42–56.

Goldberg, D.T., 2009. Racial comparisons, relational racisms: Some thoughts on method. *Ethnic and Racial Studies*, *32*(7), pp. 1271–1282.

Gopalakrishnan, S. and Chong, K.H., 2020. The prospect of community-led place-keeping as urban commons in public residential estates in Singapore. *Built Environment*, *46*(1), pp. 115–138.

Graham, S. and Thrift, N., 2007. Out of order: Understanding repair and maintenance. *Theory, Culture & Society*, *24*(3), pp. 1–25.

Graham, S., 2009. Cities as battlespace: The new military urbanism. *City*, *13*(4), pp. 383–402.

Graham, S., 2010a. *Cities Under Siege: The New Urban Militarism*. London: Verso.

Graham, S., 2010b. When infrastructure fails. In S. Graham (ed.), *Disrupted Cities*. London: Routledge, pp. 1–26.

Graham, S., 2018. Elite avenues: Flyovers, freeways and the politics of urban mobility. *City*, *22*(4), pp. 527–550.

Greenspan, A., 2021. QR codes and the sentient city. *Studia Neophilologica*, *93*(2), pp. 206–218.

Guma, P.K., Akallah, J.A. and Odeo, J.O.I., 2023. Plug-in urbanism: City building and the parodic guise of new infrastructure in Africa. *Urban Studies*, *60*(13), pp. 2550–2563.

Gupta, K., Roy, A., Luthra, K. and Maithani, S., 2016. GIS based analysis for assessing the accessibility at hierarchical levels of urban green spaces. *Urban Forestry & Urban Greening*, *18*: 198–211.

Hagman, O., 2006. Morning queues and parking problems. On the broken promises of the automobile. *Mobilities*, *1*(1), pp. 63–74.

Han, H., 2017. Singapore, a garden city: Authoritarian environmentalism in a developmental state. *The Journal of Environment & Development*, *26*(1), pp. 3–24.

Harris, E., 2015. Navigating pop-up geographies: Urban space–times of flexibility, interstitiality and immersion. *Geography Compass*, *9*(11), pp. 592–603.

Harris, T., 2021. Air pressure: Temporal hierarchies in Nepali aviation. *Cultural Anthropology*, *36*(1), pp. 83–109.

Hayes, B., 2005/2014. *Infrastructure: A Guide to the Industrial Landscape*, 2nd Edition. New York: W. W. Norton.

Henderson, J.C., 2013. Urban parks and green spaces in Singapore. *Managing Leisure*, *18*(3), pp. 213–225.

Henricks, T.S., 2015. *Play and the Human Condition*. Urbana, IL: University of Illinois Press.

Heslop, L., and Murton, G., 2021. Why Highways Remake Hierarchies. In L. Heslop and G. Muron (eds), *Highways and Hierarchies: Ethnographies of Mobility from the Himalaya to the Indian Ocean*. Amsterdam: Amsterdam University Press, pp. 21–38.

Hollett, T. and Vivoni, F., 2021. DIY Skateparks as temporary disruptions to neoliberal cities: Informal learning through micropolitical making. *Discourse: Studies in the Cultural Politics of Education*, *42*(6), pp. 881–897.

Holston, J., 2007. *Insurgent Citizenship: Disjunctions of Democracy and Modernity in Brazil*. Princeton, NJ: Princeton University Press.

Hou, J., 2010. (Not) your everyday public space. In J. Hou (ed.), *Insurgent Public Space: Guerrilla Urbanism and the Remaking of Contemporary Cities*. New York, NY: Routledge, pp. 1–18.

Howell, O., 2005. The "creative class" and the gentrifying city: Skateboarding in Philadelphia's Love Park. *Journal of Architectural Education*, *59*(2), pp. 32–42.

Huang, W., 2017. The Tripartite origins of Shenzhen: Beijing, Hong Kong, and Bao'an. In M.A. O'Donnell, W. Wong and J. Bach (eds), *Learning From Shenzhen: China's Post-Mao Experiment From Special Zone To Model City*. Chicago, IL: University of Chicago Press, pp. 65–85.

Huizinga, J., 1955. *A Study of the Play Element in Culture*. Boston: Beacon.

Hunt, G. [Dir.], 2021. *Nice to See You*. Vans. Available at: https://www.youtube.com/watch?v=A4CcloyO2mE. Accessed 12 December 2021.

Hyra, D., 2017. *Race, Class and Politics in the Cappuccino City*. Chicago: University of Chicago Press.

Ingersoll, R., 2006. *Sprawltown: Looking for the City on its Edges*. New York: Princeton Architectural Press.

Isin, E. and Ruppert, E., 2020. The birth of sensory power: How a pandemic made it visible?. *Big Data & Society*, *7*(2), p. 2053951720969208.

Iveson, K., 2010. The wars on graffiti and the new military urbanism. *City*, *14*(1–2), pp. 115–134.

Jabareen, Y. and Switat, O., 2019. Insurgent informality: The struggle over space production between the Israeli state and its Palestinian Bedouin communities. *Space and Polity*, *23*(1), pp. 92–113.

Jenks, M., 2003. Above and below the line: Globalization and urban form in Bangkok. *The Annals of Regional Science*, *37*, pp. 547–557.

Jensen, O.B., 2016. New 'Foucaultdian boomerangs': Drones and urban surveillance. *Surveillance and Society*, *14*(1), pp. 20–33.

Jiow, H.J. and Morales, S., 2015. Lateral surveillance in Singapore. *Surveillance & Society*, *13*(3/4), pp. 327–337.

Kaur, R., 2016. The innovative Indian: Common man and the politics of jugaad culture. *Contemporary South Asia*, *24*(3), pp. 313–327.

Kazmi, H., Mehmood, F., Tao, Z., Riaz, Z. and Driesen, J., 2019. Electricity load-shedding in Pakistan: Unintended consequences, opportunities and policy recommendations. *Energy Policy*, *128*, pp. 411–417.

Kennedy, L. and Sood, A., 2016. Greenfield development as "Tabula Rasa": Rescaling, speculation and governance on India's urban frontier. *Economic and Political Weekly*, *51*(17), pp. 41–49.

Kikon, D. and McDuie-Ra, D., 2021. *Ceasefire City: Militarism, Capitalism, and Urbanism in Dimapur*. New Delhi: Oxford University Press.

Kitchin, R., 2014. The real-time city? Big data and smart urbanism. *GeoJournal*, *79*, pp. 1–14.

Klauser, F., 2013. Spatialities of security and surveillance: Managing spaces, separations and circulations at sport mega events. *Geoforum*, *49*, pp. 289–298.

Klauser, F., 2017. *Surveillance and Space*. Thousand Oaks, CA: Sage.

Krim, A., 1992. Los Angeles and the anti-tradition of the suburban city. *Journal of Historical Geography, 18*(1), pp. 121–138.

Kumar, A., 2021. Between metis and techne: Politics, possibilities and limits of improvisation. *Social & Cultural Geography, 22*(6), pp. 783–806.

Kyrönviita, M. and Wallin, A., 2022. Building a DIY skatepark and doing politics hands-on. *City, 26*(4), pp. 646–663.

Laskey, A.B. and Nicholls, W., 2019. Jumping off the ladder: Participation and insurgency in Detroit's urban planning. *Journal of the American Planning Association, 85*(3), pp. 348–362.

Lederman, J., 2020. *Chasing World-class Urbanism: Global Policy versus Everyday Survival in Buenos Aires*. Minneapolis, MN: University of Minnesota Press.

Lee, T. and Lee, H., 2023. Bodily surveillance: Singapore's COVID-19 app and technological opportunism. *Continuum, 37*(5), pp. 621–634.

Lemanski, C., 2020. Infrastructural citizenship: The everyday citizenships of adapting and/or destroying public infrastructure in Cape Town, South Africa. *Transactions of the Institute of British Geographers, 45*(3), pp. 589–605.

Long Live Southbank. 2021. *Space and Why it Matters*. London: Long Live Southbank. Available at: https://www.llsb.com/pdf/space-and-why-it-matters-v4.pdf. Accessed 6 August, 2022.

López-Calvo, I., 2011. *Latino Los Angeles in Film and Fiction: The Cultural Production of Social Anxiety*. Tucson, AZ: University of Arizona Press.

Lorr, M., 2005. Skateboarding and the X-gamer phenomenon: A case of subcultural cooptation. *Humanity & Society, 29*(2), pp. 140–147.

Loukaitou-Sideris, A. and Ehrenfeucht, R., 2011. *Sidewalks: Conflict and Negotiation over Public Space*. Cambridge: MIT Press.

Low, S.M., 1997. Urban public spaces as representations of culture: The plaza in Costa Rica. *Environment and Behavior, 29*(1), pp. 3–33.

Lund, C., 2021. *Nine-tenths of the Law: Enduring Dispossession in Indonesia*. New Haven, CT: Yale University Press.

Luque-Ayala, A. and Marvin, S., 2016. The maintenance of urban circulation: An operational logic of infrastructure control. *Environment and Planning D: Society and Space, 34*(2), pp. 191–208.

Lyon, D., 2007. *Surveillance Studies: An Overview*. Cambridge: Polity.

Lyon, D., 2018. *The Culture of Surveillance: Watching as a Way of Life*. Cambridge: Polity.

Maalsen, S., 2022. The hack: What it is and why it matters to urban studies. *Urban Studies, 59*(2), pp. 453–465.

Madanipour, A., 2018. Temporary use of space: Urban processes between flexibility, opportunity and precarity. *Urban Studies, 55*(5), pp. 1093–1110.

Mäkinen, L.A., 2016. Surveillance on/off: Examining home surveillance systems from the user's perspective. *Surveillance & Society, 14*(1), pp. 59–77.

Mare, A., 2020. Internet shutdowns in Africa| state-ordered internet shutdowns and digital authoritarianism in Zimbabwe. *International Journal of Communication, 14*, p. 20.

Martin, P., 2013. Embodiment in skateboarding videogames. *International Journal of Performance Arts and Digital Media, 9*(2), pp. 315–327.

Martin, M., Hincks, S. and Deas, I., 2020. Temporary use in England's core cities: Looking beyond the exceptional. *Urban Studies, 57*(16), pp. 3381–3401.

Mattern, S., 2017. *Code and Clay, Data and Dirt: Five Thousand Years of Urban Media.* Minneapolis, MN: University of Minnesota Press.

Mattern, S., 2018. Maintenance and care. *Places Journal.* Available at: https://placesjournal .org/article/maintenance-and-care/?msclkid=7ef26afed03911eca225af3c1d3b52f0

Matyczyk, E., 2022. Power, play, and the everyday: Akademia Ruchu's Cold War street performances. *Public Art Dialogue, 12*(1), pp. 24–42.

Mbembe, A., 2017. *The Critique of Black Reason.* Translated by L. Dubois. Durham, NC: Duke: University Press.

McDonald, W. [Dir.], 2024. *Rowan Davis: Bin Kicker.* Free Skateboard Magazine. Available at: https://www.youtube.com/watch?v=r1vbon26-lc. Accessed 4 June 2024.

McDowell, L., 1983. Towards an understanding of the gender division of urban space. *Environment and planning D: Society and Space, 1*(1), pp. 59–72.

McDuie-Ra, D., 2016. *Borderland City in New India.* Amsterdam: Amsterdam University Press.

McDuie-Ra, D., 2021a. *Skateboarding and Urban Landscapes in Asia: Endless Spots.* Amsterdam: Amsterdam University Press.

McDuie-Ra, D., 2021b. *Skateboard Video: Archiving the City from Below.* Singapore: Springer.

McDuie-Ra, D., 2023a. Racial diversity in skateboarding: Destabilising whiteness, decentring heartlands. *Sport in Society, 26*(11), pp. 1802–1819.

McDuie-Ra, D., 2023b. Skateboarding in the empty city: A radical archive of alternative pandemic mobilities. *Mobilities, 18*(5), pp. 821–838.

McDuie-Ra, D., Robinson, D.F. and Gulson, K.N., 2024. Pandemic surveillance and mobilities across Sydney, New South Wales. *Geographical Research, 62*(1), pp. 45–57.

McFarlane, C., 2011. Assemblage and critical urbanism. *City, 15*(2), pp. 204-224.

Mehta, V., 2022. *Public Space: Notes on Why it Matters, What We Should Know, and How to Realize its Potential.* New York, NY: Routledge.

Meth, P., 2010. Unsettling insurgency: Reflections on women's insurgent practices in South Africa. *Planning Theory & Practice, 11*(2), pp. 241–263.

Miaux, S. and Garneau, J., 2016. The sports park and urban promenade in the 'quais de Bordeaux': An example of sports and recreation in urban planning. *Loisir et société/ Society and Leisure, 39*(1), pp. 12–30.

Miraftab, F., 2009. Insurgent planning: Situating radical planning in the global south. *Planning Theory, 8*(1), pp. 32–50.

Mohl, R.A., 2012. The expressway teardown movement in American cities: Rethinking postwar highway policy in the post-interstate era. *Journal of Planning History, 11*(1), pp. 89–103.

Mould, O., 2015. *Urban Subversion and the Creative City.* London: Routledge.

Müller, M. and Trubina, E., 2020. Improvising urban spaces, inhabiting the in-between. *Environment and Planning D: Society and Space, 38*(4), pp. 664–681.

Murphet, J., 2001. *Literature and Race in Los Angeles.* Cambridge: Cambridge University Press.

Narayan, S., 2023. CCTVs and the criminal city. *Surveillance & Society, 21*(4), pp. 363–374.

Nawratek, K. and Mehan, A., 2020. De-colonizing public spaces in Malaysia: Dating in Kuala Lumpur. *Cultural Geographies, 27*(4), pp. 615–629.

Nethercote, M., 2018. Theorising vertical urbanisation. *City, 22*(5–6), pp. 657–684.

Nijholt, A., 2017. *Playable Cities: The City as a Digital Playground.* Singapore: Springer.

O'Callaghan, J., Hogben, P. and Freestone, R., 2016. Introduction. In J. O'Callaghan, P. Hogben, and R. Freestone (eds), *Sydney's Martin Place: A Cultural and Design History*. Crow's Nest: Allen and Unwin, pp. 26–66.

O'Connor, P., 2018. Beyond the youth culture: Understanding middle-aged skateboarders through temporal capital. *International Review for the Sociology of Sport, 53*(8), pp. 924–943.

O'Connor, P., 2024. Conceptualising grey spaces in skateboarding: Generating theory and method for use beyond the board. *International Review for the Sociology of Sport, 59*(7), pp. 957–974. https://doi.org/10126902241250089.

O'Connor, P., Evers, C., Glenney, B. and Willing, I., 2023. Skateboarding in the Anthropocene: Grey spaces of polluted leisure. *Leisure Studies, 42*(6), pp. 897–907.

O'Keeffe, P. and Jenkins, L.F., 2022. "Keep your wheels off the furniture": The marginalization of street skateboarding in the City of Melbourne's "Skate Melbourne Plan". *Space and Culture*. https://doi.org/10.12063312221096015.

Pearce, C., 2009. *Communities of Play: Emergent Cultures in Multiplayer Games and Virtual Worlds*. Cambridge MA; MIT Press.

Pingel, T.J., 2018. Using web maps to analyze the construction of global scale cognitive maps. *Journal of Geography, 117*(4), pp. 153–164.

Rigolon, A., Browning, M. and Jennings, V., 2018. Inequities in the quality of urban park systems: An environmental justice investigation of cities in the United States. *Landscape and Urban Planning, 178*, pp. 156–169.

Ritchie, M., 2020. Fusing race: The phobogenics of racializing surveillance. *Surveillance & Society, 18*(1), pp. 12–29.

Rosenberger, R., 2023. A classification scheme for hostile design. *Philosophy of the City Journal, 1*(1), pp. 49–70.

Roy, A., 2011. Slumdog cities: Rethinking subaltern urbanism. *International Journal of Urban and Regional Research, 35*(2), pp. 223–238.

Ruddick, S., 1996. Constructing difference in public spaces: Race, class, and gender as interlocking systems. *Urban Geography, 17*(2), pp. 132–151.

Rupp, S., 2016. Circuits and currents: Dynamics of disruption in New York City blackouts. *Economic Anthropology, 3*(1), pp. 106–118.

Sahoo, S., 2023. India's internet shutdowns as biopolitics: The formation of political will and opinion through collective action under attack. *Critical Studies in Media Communication, 40*(5), pp. 291–305.

Schwinghammer, S., 2020. Leo Valls Interview. *Solo Skate Mag*. Available at: https://soloskatemag.com/leo-valls-interview. Accessed 3 November 2021.

Shatkin, G., 2014. Reinterpreting the meaning of the 'Singapore Model': State capitalism and urban planning. *International Journal of Urban and Regional Research, 38*(1), pp. 116–137.

Shepard, B., 2012. *Play, Creativity, and Social Movements: If I Can't Dance, It's Not My Revolution*. New York, NY: Routledge.

Shields, R., 2013. *Spatial Questions: Cultural Topologies and Social Spatialisations*. London: Sage.

Shih, M. and Chiang, Y.H., 2022. A politically less contested and financially more calculable urban future: Density techniques and heightened land commodification in Taiwan. *Environment and Planning A: Economy and Space, 56*(6), pp. 1753–1770.

Shusterman, R., 1999. Somaesthetics: A disciplinary proposal. *The Journal of Aesthetics and Art Criticism, 57*(3), pp. 299–313.

Sicart, M., 2014. *Play Matters*. Cambridge, MA: MIT Press.

Simon, K., 2016. Animating public space. In J. O'Callaghan, P. Hogben, and R. Freestone (eds), *Sydney's Martin Place: A Cultural and Design History*. Crow's Nest: Allen and Unwin, pp. 441–474.

Smith, N. and Walters, P., 2018. Desire lines and defensive architecture in modern urban environments. *Urban Studies*, *55*(13), pp. 2980–2995.

Snyder, G.J., 2017. *Skateboarding LA: Inside Professional Street Skateboarding*. New York: New York University Press.

Solomon, H., 2021. Death traps: Holes in urban India. *Environment and Planning D: Society and Space*, *39*(3), pp. 423–440.

Sood, A., 2015. Industrial townships and the policy facilitation of corporate urbanisation in India. *Urban Studies*, *52*(8), pp. 1359–1378.

Stelzer, J., 2023. The seriousness of play: Johan Huizinga's Homo Ludens and the demise of the play-element. *International Journal of Play*, *12*(3), pp. 337–348.

Stevens, N. and Keyes, O., 2021. Seeing infrastructure: Race, facial recognition and the politics of data. *Cultural Studies*, *35*(4–5), pp.833–853.

Stevens, Q., 2007. *The Ludic City: Exploring the Potential of Public Spaces*. London: Routledge.

Stoetzer, B., 2018. Ruderal ecologies: Rethinking nature, migration, and the urban landscape in Berlin. *Cultural Anthropology*, *33*(2), pp. 295–323.

Summers, B.T., 2022. Black insurgent aesthetics and the public imaginary. *Urban Geography*, *43*(6), pp. 837–847.

Sutton-Smith, B., 1997. *The Ambiguity of Play*. Cambridge, MA: Harvard University

Thorpe, H. and Wheaton, B., 2011. 'Generation X Games', action sports and the Olympic movement: Understanding the cultural politics of incorporation. *Sociology*, *45*(5), pp. 830–847.

Throop, C.J. and Duranti, A., 2015. Attention, ritual glitches, and attentional pull: The president and the queen. *Phenomenology and the Cognitive Sciences*, *14*, pp. 1055–1082.

Throop, C.J., 2018. Being open to the world. *HAU: Journal of Ethnographic Theory*, *8*(1–2), pp. 197–210.

Truelove, Y., 2021. Gendered infrastructure and liminal space in Delhi's unauthorized colonies. *Environment and Planning D: Society and Space*, *39*(6), pp. 1009–1025.

UNHABITAT., 2018. *SDG Indicator 11.7.1 Training Module: Public Space*. United Nations Human Settlement Programme (UN-Habitat), Nairobi.

United Nations Department of Economic and Social Affairs, UN DESA., n.d. Sustainable Development Goals 11.7. Available at: https://sdgs.un.org/goals/goal11#targets_and _indicators. Accessed 6 July 2024.

United Nations Department of Economic and Social Affairs, UN DESA., 2023. Progress and Info. Available at: https://sdgs.un.org/goals/goal11#progress_and_info. Accessed 12 April 2024.

Venter, Z.S., Shackleton, C.M., Van Staden, F., Selomane, O. and Masterson, V.A., 2020. Green Apartheid: Urban green infrastructure remains unequally distributed across income and race geographies in South Africa. *Landscape and Urban Planning*, *203*, p. 103889.

Vivoni, F., 2013. Waxing ledges: Built environments, alternative sustainability, and the Chicago skateboarding scene. *Local Environment*, *18*(3), pp. 340–353.

Wallius, E., Thibault, M., Apperley, T. and Hamari, J., 2022. Gamifying the city: E-scooters and the critical tensions of playful urban mobility. *Mobilities*, *17*(1), pp. 85–101.

Walz, S.P., 2010. *Toward a Ludic Architecture: The Space of Play and Games*. Pittsburgh, PA: ETC Press.

Warin, R., 2018. Long Live Southbank: Skateboarding, citizenship and the city. *The Journal of Public Space*, *3*(3), pp. 149–158.

Williams, N., 2020. Colour in the lines: The racial politics and possibilities of US skateboarding culture. PhD Thesis, University of Waikato.

Williams, N., 2022. Before the gold: Connecting aspirations, activism, and BIPOC excellence through Olympic skateboarding. *Journal of Olympic Studies*, *3*(1), pp. 4–27.

Willing, I., Bennett, A., Piispa, M. and Green, B., 2019. Skateboarding and the 'tired generation': Ageing in youth cultures and lifestyle sports. *Sociology*, *53*(3), pp. 503–518.

Wu, L. and Kim, S.K., 2021. Exploring the equality of accessing urban green spaces: A comparative study of 341 Chinese cities. *Ecological Indicators*, *121*, p. 107080.

Wylie, J., 2006. Depths and folds: On landscape and the gazing subject. *Environment and Planning D: Society and Space*, *24*(4), pp. 519–535.

Yeo, S.J.I., 2023. Smart urban living in Singapore? Thinking through everyday geographies. *Urban Geography*, *44*(4), pp. 687–706.

Yochim, E.C., 2009. *Skate Life: Re-Imagining White Masculinity*. Ann Arbor: University of Michigan Press.

Young, A., 2013. *Street Art, Public City: Law, Crime and the Urban Imagination*. London: Routledge.

Zou, D.V., 2010. A historical study of the 'Zo' struggle. *Economic and Political Weekly*, *45*(14), pp. 56–63.

Zugayar, M., Avni, N. and Silverman, E., 2021. Vertical informality: The case of Kufr Aqab in east Jerusalem. *Land Use Policy*, *105*, p. 105395.

INDEX

www.ingramcontent.com/pod-product-compliance
Lightning Source LLC
Chambersburg PA
CBHW031446280326
41927CB00037B/368